Approaches to Art
Teachers Resource Book

Key Stage Two
(P4-7)

Anthea Peppin, Ray Smith and Ailsa Turner

Acknowledgements

The publishers wish to thank the following for permission to reproduce the pictures in this book:

Pictures 1, 10, 12, 27, 35 Reproduced by Courtesy of the Trustees of the British Museum; **Picture 2** Glasgow Museums, Art Gallery and Museum, Kelvingrove; **Picture 3** Musées Royaux des Beaux-Arts de Belgiques, Brussels; **Pictures 4, 13, 24, 25, 38** Reproduced by Courtesy of the Trustees, The National Gallery, London; **Picture 5** Osterreichische Nationalbibliothek, Vienna; **Picture 6** National Archaeological Museum, Athens; **Picture 7** © Henry Moore Foundation (1993). Reproduced by kind permission of the Henry Moore Foundation; **Picture 8** The Bard, Laing Art Gallery, Newcastle-upon-Tyne (Tyne and Wear Museums); **Picture 9** Ashmolean Museum, Oxford; **Picture 11** Courtesy of Marlborough Fine Art (London) Ltd; **Picture 14** Kunsthistorisches Museum, Vienna; **Picture 15** National Portrait Gallery, London; **Pictures 16, 17** Yale Center for British Art, Paul Mellon Collection, New Haven, Connecticut; **Picture 18** The Jean Pigozzi Contemporary African Art Collection; **Picture 19** Bibliothèque Nationale, Paris; **Picture 20** Rijksmuseum, Amsterdam; **Picture 21** Lee Boltin Picture Libary, New York; **Picture 22** The Library of Congress, Washington D.C./Bridgeman Art Library; **Picture 23** Gemäldegalerie Neue Meister, Staatliche Kunstsammlungen, Dresden; **Picture 26** Katsushika Hokusai, Wild Sea at Chōshi, Musée de Guimet © Photo R.M.N.; **Picture 28** Kelmscott Manor/Bridgeman Art Library; **Picture 29** Eugène Delacroix, Interior of Moroccan House, The Louvre © Photo R.M.N.; **Picture 30** The Tate Gallery, London; **Picture 31** Courtesy of the artist, Bill Woodrow; **Picture 32** © The Phillips Collection, Washington D.C. Joan Miró, The Red Sun 1948 © ADAGP, Paris and DACS, London 1993; **Picture 33** Photo: SCALA, Florence; **Picture 34** Paul Cézanne, Pommes Vertes, The Louvre © Photo R.M.N.; **Picture 36** The Linares family © Documentation du Musée National d'Art Moderne – Centre Georges Pompidou, Paris. Photo: B. Hatala; **Picture 37** Courtesy of Anthony d'Offay Gallery; **Picture 39** Add Ms 42130 fol. 59v. Reproduced by Courtesy of the British Library; **Picture 40** Gift of Henry H. Marquand 1889. Copyright © 1993 by the Metropolitan Museum of Art, New York; **Picture 41** The Royal Academy of Arts, London.

Artists: Cindy Wonnacott pp. 159, 160, Hardlines Illustration and Design pp. 78, 118, 150, 151, 152, 153, 154, 156, 157, 158, Ray Smith p. 155.

Published by Ginn and Company Ltd
Prebendal House, Parson's Fee, Aylesbury
Bucks HP20 2QZ

Printed in Great Britain by Page Bros, Norwich
Typeset by Artistix, Tetsworth, Oxon

Contents

1. Art and the National Curriculum

The National Curriculum in Art became statutory in England for pupils in Years 1 and 3 in September 1992 and applies to all other pupils from September 1993. In Scotland, Art and Design come under the umbrella of the Expressive Arts 5-14, guidelines for which were introduced in Autumn 1992.

Content of the Art curriculum for England

The curriculum in Art in England is structured around two Attainment Targets: *AT1: Investigating and Making* and *AT2: Knowledge and Understanding*.

AT1 is defined as 'The development of visual perception and the skills associated with investigating and making in art, craft and design.' This Attainment Target is centred around children's practical work; the added dimension 'investigating' requires children to collect, refer to and use a wide variety of visual stimuli as a basis for their own practical work.

AT2 is defined as 'The development of visual literacy and knowledge and understanding of art, craft and design including the history of art, our diverse artistic heritage and a variety of other artistic traditions together with the ability to make practical connections between this and pupils' own work.' This may seem at first sight a tall order for primary pupils; in Chapter 2 we discuss how the particular requirements for this Attainment Target at Key Stage Two can be met.

In the Statutory Orders, each Attainment Target is subdivided, for each Key Stage into End of Key Stage Statements. Related to these are individual Programmes of Study which break down the curriculum into smaller content areas; each Programme of Study has related examples to give teachers an idea of the type of activity pupils might do.

These examples are random and are not meant, in any way, to be prescriptive: thus the appearance of certain artists' names or specific themes has no significant meaning.

End of Key Stage Statement (b) (AT2 KS2) plus related Programme of Study item and example:

END OF KEY STAGE STATEMENT (b)	PROGRAMME OF STUDY (item iv)	EXAMPLE
Pupils should be able to begin to identify the characteristics of art in a variety of genres, cultures and traditions, showing some knowledge of the related historical background.	Identify and compare some of the methods and materials that artists use.	Compare the way that different artists have carved or constructed figures using materials such as stone, clay, plaster, wire; e.g. the work of Michelangelo, Epstein, Hepworth, and Giacometti.

There is strong advice throughout the Orders and previous documents that the two Attainment Targets should be taught together and not in isolation: so children's knowledge should inform their practical work and conversely they should look at other artists' work in the light of what they have made. The Ginn resources, described in detail in Chapter 2, are designed to integrate the two Attainment Targets. The Secretary of State for Education has weighted the Attainment Targets two to one in favour of AT1: Investigating and Making.

Content of the Art Curriculum for Scotland

The Art and Design Curriculum within the Expressive Arts 5-14 Guidelines divides the curriculum into Attainment Outcomes and Programmes of Study. There are three key Attainment Outcomes which are subdivided into Strands to represent key aspects of the curriculum.

OUTCOMES	STRANDS
USING Materials, Techniques, Skills and Media	Investigating visually and recording Using media Using visual elements
EXPRESSING Feelings, Ideas, Thoughts and Solutions	Creating and designing Communicating
EVALUATING AND **APPRECIATING**	Observing, reflecting, describing and responding

Because the Scottish guidelines are much more detailed than the English equivalent it has not been possible to provide precise references to both curricula in Chapters 5 and 6. These chapters are therefore referenced only to the English National Curriculum. **Detailed correlation and record sheets will be available separately for Scottish schools.**

There is, however, a great deal of common ground and similar emphasis within the two curricula and *Approaches to Art* is designed to resource both curricula.

For example, the emphasis on recording from observation (Scottish Strand: Investigating visually and recording), the use of a wide range of materials, techniques, skills and media (Scottish Strand: Using media) are common to both curricula. Both curricula emphasise the importance of developing a visual vocabulary (see Using visual elements – Scottish Programme of Study, Levels C and D and page 8 below). Cross curricular approaches (see Chapter 5) are encouraged and a similar emphasis is placed on planning, reviewing and modifying work; there is similar emphasis on the use of source materials and of course on the development of the elements of art: colour, tone, line, texture, pattern and form (Strands: Using visual elements and Creating and designing). Both curricula also include the requirement that children should relate their work to that of other artists and designers (Strand: Observing, reflecting, describing and responding).

The referencing to the English Programmes of Study in Chapters 5 and 6 clearly identify which elements of the curriculum mentioned above are being focused upon throughout the suggested Discussion questions and Activities in this book.

2. Approaches to Art: Delivering the National Curriculum

The Approaches to Art materials

Approaches to Art has been designed to provide materials to help teachers deliver the requirements of the National Curriculum for Years 1-6 or the Art and Design 5-14 Guidelines for P1-7. The materials comprise large format Group Discussion Books and related Teachers' Resource Books – one set aimed broadly at Key Stage One (P1-3) and this set designed for children in Key Stage Two (P4-7). The books are not designed as a prescriptive programme to be followed sequentially but as a flexible collection of ideas to augment the practical work that children are already doing in the classroom.

The aim of the materials is particularly to resource the areas of the Art curriculum that might be new to teachers and the ones that otherwise would be time-consuming and difficult to resource comprehensively.

The Group Discussion Books

The Group Discussion Books bring together a very wide and varied collection of works of art. Their aim is to provide images for children to talk about – both to build their knowledge and understanding (AT2) and to act as stimuli for their own work (AT1). This book includes a wide range of two-dimensional art and craft work, with examples of painting, photography, drawing, printing, calligraphy and weaving in addition to three-dimensional sculpture and craft work including carved, modelled and constructed works in various materials, pottery and metalwork.

We had two key aims in the exhaustive search for images for this book: firstly to choose images that 7-11 year olds could relate to and enjoy; our experience working with children in schools and in the National Gallery helped enormously here. Secondly, to meet the curriculum requirements, we needed to provide a collection of images chosen from many cultures and across time. A quick glance at the picture summary on page 0 will show the variety of sources both in terms of country and in terms of time – from the 6th century B.C. to 1991-2.

To augment the collection of pictures and to have more material to compare and contrast, teachers can make use of the other *Approaches to Art Group Discussion Book*, published for Key Stage One. References to that book are included, where appropriate, in the discussion or activity sections in Chapter 6 in this book.

From discussion of this range of images children will start to be aware of the variety of art in terms of genre, period, culture and tradition.

The NC document (KS2 AT2 Pos iii) states that children should 'look at and discuss art from early, Renaissance and later periods in order to understand the way in which art has developed and the contribution of influential artists or groups of artists to that development'. Obviously it depends how you interpret such a statement but it does sound like an alarmingly tall order. It could mean that children should at this stage be given a thorough grounding in the entire history of art! The use of the word 'developed' here is curious also – as it implies a progressive improvement in art over the centuries, which is far from what actually happened. There are problems too with the idea of 'influential' artists being the ones which should be studied. Some artists who were very influential in their own day are virtually unknown today – largely due to accidents of history. An example is Carel Fabritius, perhaps the most brilliant of Rembrandt's pupils, and much admired in his own day. Not only did he die young when a gunpowder store in Delft blew up in 1654, but most of his paintings were destroyed at the same time. Other artists who were not particularly influential in their own lifetime have become so later, for example, the post impressionist painter Seurat studied pictures by the Renaissance artist Piero della Francesca. Other artists who were spectacularly brilliant at their craft are known only by their works – their names have been lost. Quite a number of the images in this book are of artefacts by such unknown artists. We chose them because of the quality of the work, not because we had heard of the person who did them. Things such as ancient sculpture and jewellery and medieval manuscripts and objects fall into this category.

The most important point to bear in mind is that you do not have to be an art historian or an artist to look at art. You don't have to know the name of who did it, or when or where it was done to enjoy looking at it and learn from doing so. Your pupils, by looking at all sorts of images, and discussing intelligently what they see, will become visually literate, will know how to approach the process of looking and will pick up a sense of style and history in a enjoyable and painless way.

The Teachers' Resources

The main purpose of these Teachers' Resources is to provide teachers with suggestions for practical art activities to cover all the requirements laid out in the Statutory Orders for England and Scotland. These are contained in Chapter 6 of this book. Each picture in the Group Discussion Book has a separate section in Chapter 6 of this book structured as follows: firstly, for the teacher, there is background information about the work of art and its artist; secondly, we have included suggestions on how to structure the discussion of the picture with the class. In our experience, finding fruitful questions to ask is often the most difficult task for non-specialists, particularly with young children. Our daily experience with children visiting the National Gallery has helped formulate appropriate questions and directions for discussion. (Further guidance on looking at pictures with young children is given in Chapter 3.)

Our particular aim in writing the discussion questions in this book has been to help build children's concepts, knowledge and understanding of art. Particular questions might be more suitable for discussion with 10 and 11 year olds who will bring a greater knowledge and conceptual understanding to the discussion. Our intention has also been to broaden the areas of discussion to include consideration of the context of the picture as well as talking about the picture itself.

Following these discussion sections, are suggestions for practical activities. These are designed to cover particular aspects of the Programmes of Study. For example, the activities for Picture 18, the African funerary sculpture, focus on resourcing AT1 POS ii, 'respond to memory and the imagination using a range of media'; POS iv, 'experiment with ideas suggested by different source materials and explain how they have used them to develop their work' and POS x, 'plan and make three-dimensional structures using various materials and for a variety of purposes'.

The practical activities also contain suggestions that include ideas for individual, group and class work and for working in two and three dimensions, in order to fulfil the General Requirements of the Statutory Orders.

At the beginning of the description of each picture we have noted the particular parts of the Programme of Study for AT1 that the activities focus upon.

Only AT1 POS i-x are referred to because we feel that the requirements of AT1 POS xi and xii and the POS for AT2 cannot be met by specific activities related to individual pictures but will be met by cumulative working through a variety of activities over the four years in the Key Stage. Suggestions for monitoring coverage of AT2 are given in Chapter 5, Planning Units of Work.

We have also, at the beginning of each section in Chapter 6, included a note of special art-focused and cross curricular topics that the discussion and activities fit in with – see Using the materials.

Developing a specialist vocabulary

It is important to recognise that children have to develop a conceptual vocabulary that actually allows them to talk about art, craft and design in a meaningful way. They must learn to get away from simply expressing their ideas about a piece of art in terms of personal preferences. They need to build up a specialist vocabulary that will allow them to address seriously the processes by which different artists at different times and in different cultures have made their work.

Now, one of the Statutory requirements at this Key Stage (AT1 POS xii; Scottish POS Level C/D, Strand Using visual elements) is for children to begin to develop a specialist vocabulary to describe their work; children are also required to 'understand and use subject-specific terms, such as landscape, still life, mural' (AT2 POS ii). In all our background information and discussion sections we have introduced and explained appropriate artistic terms and vocabulary so that teachers can readily introduce and familiarise children with them. These words are printed in bold. If we pay attention to this very important area of discourse, we way and that art will begin to mean a great deal more to them.

Using the materials

It is clear that, with the pressure on time already in the primary curriculum, teachers are not going to have extra time to spend on art. The background to the Final Report of the Art Working Group suggests that on average one hour and forty minutes a week is spent on art at Key Stage Two.

We would see much art arising out of other work in the classroom – either linked to topic or subject-specific activities. Our resources are designed to be used in any order and to be used selectively; the cross curricular links or the subject of the work of art itself may be the most appropriate way of choosing a suitable picture to talk about.

Once you have selected a particular picture or pictures to discuss you will need to choose which practical activity you are going to do as a follow up and prepare the materials required beforehand. (A note on practical work and materials is included in Chapter 4.) The practical activities offer several alternatives to choose from. It is not suggested that children attempt more than one. Much will depend on whether a group, class or individual activity is to be selected. It may well be, of course, that you begin with some practical work and then proceed to a discussion of one of the pictures. This will illuminate what the children have started doing before they continue with it in the light of the discussion.

Try to guide the latter parts of the discussion towards the practical activity you have chosen. Sometimes you may wish to do the discussion on one day and the practical work on another – perhaps reminding the children of the image they discussed with you and how their work might lead on from this.

For teachers wishing to plan work in art in a more structured way to ensure full coverage of the National Curriculum and progression through the Key Stage, we have provided suggestions for planning units of work based around our collection of pictures and focusing on particular themes to resource specific areas of the art curriculum. See Chapter 5 for details. In this chapter we also outline ideas for incorporating the art activities into cross curricular topic work – particularly in English, History, Geography and Technology.

Recording and assessment

The Art Non-Statutory Guidance states that assessment should be based on the End of Key Stage Statements. As there are no levels in Art there will not be an AT score; instead 'descriptive judgements are required which are based on accumulated evidence'; 'record keeping should be kept to a minimum and should be sufficient to track curriculum progress'. Currently there are no Statutory requirements for classroom assessment at the end of the Key Stages. However, many teachers will want to track children's coverage of the curriculum to ensure progression throughout the Key Stage. The Non-Statutory Guidance provides examples of how simple records can be kept; we have also provided a simple photocopiable record sheet on page 149 to help teachers using *Approaches to Art* to record pupils' coverage of the curriculum. Chapter 5 also provides guidance on planning work and progression.

Record Sheets relating to Scottish Levels B-D will be published separately.

3. Looking at pictures with young children

You do not have to be an artist or an art historian to look at art. It is something that everyone, young and old can do. By looking, thinking and asking yourself questions you can discover a lot without opening a book or even reading a label. One of the keys to looking is to ask questions about the work of art and perhaps the least interesting question (and the one which people most often think they ought to ask) is: 'who is it by?' Only experts can answer this just by looking at the work. Try instead questions like these:

What sort of person might have wanted a work of art like that?
Where might it have been put originally? (e.g. a room in a house/church/palace/public park etc.)
What is it of? (i.e. its subject matter.)
What is it meant to make you feel?
Why would an artist produce a thing like that?
What is it made of?

When looking at an image with young children – be it print or painting, sculpture or whatever – start with the obvious. What stands out? What do they notice first? If you are talking about painting this is likely to be the subject matter. Is it the naked bodies, the dragon, the pattern or whatever that stands out as the most prominent aspect of the subject? If you are talking about a three-dimensional object, after the subject matter, talk about the size, weight and the material it seems to be made of. If you can, walk round it and see what it looks like from the other side, from above and so on. Of course, if you are looking at a *photograph* of a three-dimensional object you must point that out and discuss the limitations that this two-dimensional representation imposes on you. And of course you will have to guess at what it looks like from other view points!

What is the difference between a reproduction and a real painting? One way to approach this question is to take the book of plates and ask the children 'How many paintings are there in this book?' The answer is of course 'none'. There are pictures or prints or reproductions in the book but there are no actual paintings.

What is special about the 'real thing'? You should be thinking about scale, clarity, texture, and whether it is two or three dimensional. Also age and uniqueness should be considered. Most originals are unique. They have been made by someone who will have put considerable time, effort, thought and expense into producing a 'one off'. And this may have been done several hundred years ago. The thing which the artist or craftsman produced may have been treasured for centuries by a succession of owners before ending up in a museum or gallery.

By the time they reach Key Stage Two (P4), children will start to bring their experience to bear when looking at works of art. They will be beginning to develop an awareness of complexity – and will be able to grasp ideas such as allegory and symbolism. They will also be interested in method and technique and will be keen to 'have a go' whenever possible.

However, when looking at works of art with junior children, don't take anything for granted. We as adults will have no problem in recognising gods and goddesses from Greek or Roman mythology or Christian saints or figures from history. This is because experience has given us certain expectations – we expect paintings to contain such things and we can usually recognise them when they do. Children are still developing the mental framework which will enable them to read these clues and it is up to us to show them how to do this. You can convey this idea to them by saying that looking at works of art is a bit like being a detective. Images contain clues which tell us things and we need to learn to read these clues in order to work out what is going on.

Junior children are often very perceptive and refreshingly eager to share their views. They will not necessarily have noticed all the things you have noticed, and they will certainly spot things you have missed. At this stage, as with infants, they may not interpret what they see correctly: e.g. at the National Gallery a child, seeing the figure of Juno naked in the sky in Tintoretto's 'The Origin of the Milky Way', thought that the goddess must be in a nudist camp. Another child decided that because the figure of the king in Rembrandt's 'Belshazzar's Feast' was wearing a turban, he must have just washed his hair! It is very important when errors of fact such as these arise (and they will quite often) that the teacher handles the situation with great tact. A response of 'No, that's wrong' or 'Don't be so silly' can put a child off for life.

There are many ways of discussing a picture with juniors. Listing games (which work well with infants) can still be used: each child in turn names something in or about the art work that has not been mentioned previously. You can turn this into a competition – repetition means you are 'out'. Another way of looking is for each person to think up one question which can be answered by looking at the image. Or you can use the image as a springboard for imaginative work – make up a story to fit the picture. This can be done collectively as a class discussion.

However, by the time Key Stage Two is reached, marvellous opportunities for cross curricular work arise. We cannot stress too strongly how important we think these are. After all , art, and that includes the enjoyment of other people's work, should not be confined :o a set moment in the timetable, but seen as (and we do know this is an awful cliché) part of life. We have therefore tried to suggest a few ideas for cross curricular work in this book (see Chapter 5), but we would like to emphasise that what we have suggested is really only the tip of a very large iceberg!

Think for a moment about the links to be made between **mathematics** and art for example. Both can be about shape, size, number, proportion, geometry, finance, and in some cases perspective. Or consider **geography**: you can make plans of many pictures, you can chart where they were made on a map, you can trace a work of art's movements since its creation, or the artist's travels. You can work out where certain pigments came from . . . which leads us into the world of **science**. What is (or was) paint made of? What is bronze? How does a camera work? Of course, all art works lend themselves to work in **English**. There is the matter of vocabulary extension – not just the specialist vocabulary requirements of the Art in the NC Orders – but the extended vocabulary that can arise out of a discussion of a work of art. Before embarking on such a discussion, it would be well to decide on say ten new words you intend to introduce. Of course the possibilities of using works of art as a stimulus for creative writing are almost limitless. Stories, conversations, poetry and drama for example are all obvious candidates here.

What we urge is that teachers of juniors should not feel shackled if they lack a degree in History of Art. They should feel free to plunder art works in an imaginative and creative way in order to enrich their teaching of *all* subjects.

All of these things can of course be done with reproductions. If the Real Thing is being used in a museum, gallery, country house or whatever, your discussion should include some consideration of scale and technique.

Scale: the size of the artwork is very interesting and almost invariably lost in a reproduction. You can, for example, talk about whether the people in a picture or sculpture are life-size, larger than life or smaller and, in the case of paintings, you can discuss what sort of building/person you think the work would have been done for originally (palace, house, king, ordinary person etc.).

Technique: can sometimes be discussed in connection with a reproduction. It is wise to preface your remarks in such a way that it is clear what is being said: e.g. 'we are looking at a photo of a stone statue'. However, when in front of the art work itself, what the object is made of should definitely be discussed. You can often tell what a painting is done on by looking carefully. As a general rule, European paintings that you see hanging on the walls of galleries are either done on a wood panel or on canvas. (Those done before about 1460 are almost all on wood, while those done after about 1700 are usually on canvas. Those done during the intervening years might be on either. Of course, this is an oversimplification – a fresco is painted onto wet plaster and people also paint onto copper, glass, paper and so on.) You can sometimes see the grain of wood or weave of canvas showing through the paint.

Before the mid-19th century, when pigment began to be chemically manufactured, nearly all paint was produced from naturally occurring substances such as minerals, coloured earths and organic substances such as plants and insects. The process of picture production therefore involved the preparation of a surface for painting and the making of paint as well as the actual painting of the picture. The making of a sculpture also involved various stages including perhaps a visit to a quarry to choose stone, or timber yard to choose wood.

The pictures in the Group Discussion Book which accompanies this text have been chosen because they are the sort of images that children at Key Stage Two find interesting and can relate to without too much difficulty. Nevertheless, given the limited number of images possible, we have been very careful in our selection. For example, while we know that juniors are interested in pictures of sex and violence we have deliberately avoided these. Paintings of nudes sometimes offend some religious groups and individuals. We have also avoided pictures showing excessive violence as we felt that these might deliver a confused message to the children. You should however, be prepared to encounter both of these categories when visiting galleries. We have put in a number of quite complicated works which can give rise to discussion of various interesting issues as we all know that children of this age can benefit enormously by being intellectually stretched.

One popular misconception is that children will like Impressionist paintings better than earlier art. In our experience of taking parties of children round the National Gallery this is just not the case. Brightly coloured they may be, but on the whole they lack the detail and precision that children enjoy exploring. In fact, exploration is part of the fun of looking at art – and children, used to moving images on television which are whisked away in seconds, really enjoy the opportunity to explore one picture or image in detail. We never find that young children are bored by works of art.

If, as many junior school teachers do, you decide to base a project on Art, we suggest that you do not approach this artist by artist.

Children of this age find such an approach very dull and also mildly frightening – if there is so much to find out about *this* artist and there are so many artists, how am I ever going to know it all? Also, as we said at the beginning of this chapter, *who the artist was* is perhaps the least interesting thing about a work of art. For this age group we suggest a thematic approach – images of water or the environment – for example. Taking this broader approach will offer much more scope for interesting discussion and involvement. We always feel sorry for children when a teacher tells us that his/her pupils are doing a term's work on say Monet – particularly for those in the class who don't like Monet's work!

The staff who take children round at the National Gallery often notice that a particular child has contributed to the class discussion outstandingly well only to be told later by the class teacher that the child has learning difficulties back at school. The activity of discussing art seems to have a liberating effect on these children. Those who struggle with reading or number work may have a heightened ability to 'read' pictures or other images. The process of looking and describing, away from the familiar stresses of classroom life, can be very helpful in this respect and it is worth watching out for and encouraging.

Why do we keep real paintings in special art galleries?

The answer to this – at child level – is that with old works of art the artist has often been dead many years. We have to look after the work of art because if it gets damaged or destroyed we cannot get him or her back to do another one. Old things tend to be very delicate and have to be looked after. Art galleries employ special people to do this and have special air conditioning and lighting etc. Many art galleries employ people called 'restorers' (sometimes the word 'conservator' is used, especially in the United States) who clean and repair old works of art. They also have guards to stop people from stealing or damaging the art works.

It is important for children to realise that with works of art – as with so many other things – not all the answers are known. There are lots of things which puzzle the experts. So you, as the teacher, need not be afraid of not knowing all the answers. We suggest you list the unanswerable questions that crop up in class and try to track down some of the answers later. To help you to do this we suggest the following: many museums and galleries publish catalogues which will tell you about the works in the collection. They will probably contain far more information than you need. For example, the National Gallery catalogues contain information about the artist who produced a painting, information about the painting's size, what sort of paint was used and whether it is on canvas, wood, copper or whatever. There is then a long discussion about the subject matter, the date of the picture, alterations the artist made while working on it, and so on. You are also told what other versions (if any) of the same picture exist and where they are, whether there are related works extant – for example, whether preliminary drawings by the artist survive and if so, where. You are told the provenance of the painting – i.e. where it was before it came to the gallery. This sometimes goes right back to the time when the painting was made and can be very interesting historically. You are then treated to a list of scholarly written works which mention the painting. From all of this it is possible to extract child-friendly information, but it does take some time, particularly as some catalogues do not contain illustrations! Most museum and gallery catalogues follow a similar pattern.

Other more general sources of reference information are widely available. We find *Hall's Dictionary of Subjects and Symbols in Art*, published by John Murray, particularly useful for finding out the stories in old paintings. Also *Signs and Symbols in Christian Art* by George Ferguson although the examples illustrated are unfortunately all in the United States. Penguin produce a number of useful paperback dictionaries such as the *Dictionary of Art and Artists* by Peter and Linda Murray and a *Dictionary of Saints* by D. Attwater.

Visiting museums and galleries with parties of young children

Before your visit: telephone the institution and ask what the booking procedures are. Allow about a month's notice or more – some places get very booked up so when you telephone, have several alternative dates to offer. Some galleries and museums have admission charges which will be waived if you book, some will provide a free teacher, which will have the advantage of leaving you free to make sure that you leave with the same number of children that you brought. If you book a museum or gallery teacher make sure that they are used to junior age children! If you have any children in the group who have problems (for example, sight/hearing/learning difficulties or wheelchairs) it is essential the museum teacher knows beforehand. You should also mention if there are any things which you would prefer the children not to be shown (for example, if your group is largely Muslim you may feel you should ask for them not to be shown nudes).

> Primary age children get much more out of a morning visit than an afternoon one.

> Before the visit make sure the children understand about 'gallery manners'. (Consideration for other visitors and *don't touch* are the most important.)

> Punctuality is crucial if you have booked a teacher.

> Take your children away from the museum or gallery before they have had enough rather than after. This is very important. About one to two hours is ample.

A museum or gallery teacher may not be able to tell you before you come exactly what you will be shown, so follow up work will probably be more relevant than preparation. However, if there are one or two works of art you hope they might see, a short slide-show or postcard discussion before the visit means that they might have the excitement of recognising an old friend when they arrive. Do by all means take posters and postcards (of things you have seen) back to school if the budget allows.

Visits to contemporary artists and craftspeople working in museums, residences and workshops, can also be of great interest and value.

The last and perhaps most crucial point is that any visit must be enjoyed by all (including the teacher). Children will learn more if they have a nice time and hopefully will want to go back for more. This attitude training is much more important than being able to name three artists from Ferrara or Rembrandt's dates. We must teach our children how to look and how to learn from what they see.

4. Practical work with 7-11 year olds

At the core of the National Curriculum for Art are the crucial years at Key Stage Two (P4-7). It is at this stage that pupils can so readily acquire and build on the skills, knowledge and understanding relevant to art, because they are still so receptive and genuinely interested. It is an important period of transition and development in which pupils move from the early exploration, experimentation and discovery of Key Stage One to the more mature and developed approach to art found at Key Stage Three. But within the Key Stage Two years themselves – and there are more of them than at any other Key Stage – children go through a rapid and highly significant phase of their development. The child of eleven is a far more mature and knowing person than the child of seven. Teachers need to take into account the developmental aspects of this stage of learning when they initiate practical work in association with discussion and research.

There is, of course, the link with an increasing maturity in the use of language that allows the more genuinely enquiring nature, that pupils have at this time, to express itself. They are more able to recognise and understand issues and follow an argument through its various stages. There is a focus on sequence and progression arising from a developing interest in narrative. Children at this stage are reading stories to themselves and also making them up. There are important and direct links here with art, especially in the area of pictorial narrative. In practical work, we can see their ability to envisage an end product, to set up an idea and follow it through to completion. This ties in with an increasing manual dexterity and control in the use of materials. Children are beginning to enjoy and exploit a newly acquired proficiency with the tools and materials of art. This opens up a whole new area of possibilities for practical work and it is why we think it is important, if at all possible, to provide good tools, materials and equipment at this stage. Another significant trend during this time, is an increasingly mature approach to group work, with each member of a particular team understanding how delegation works and contributing knowingly to the whole.

Although teachers need to take account of these significant aspects of pupil development at Key Stage Two, it seems to us important that any approach to the practical aspects of art is not over-complicated. Practising artists understand that a clear, simple idea may be all that is required to spark off a process of making that can result in rich and complex work. Children at this stage are quick to respond to the hugely varied possibilities of a simple idea clearly expressed and, if the teacher has a clear notion of what is expected, the pupils will invariably respond in ways that will surprise the teacher and may even surprise themselves. Pupils at this level feel comfortable with an idea when they see the point of it and are able to work more freely within its constraints. If an idea or instruction is so completely open-ended that it is difficult for pupils to recognise any of the practical possibilities that may arise from it, they will flounder and produce work of little benefit to their development.

Most of the Programmes of Study relating to End of Key Stage Two Statements for the two Attainment Targets have implications for practical work.

Researching and recording

In AT1 (or Scottish Strand: Investigating visually and recording) the aspect of visual research and the development of ideas emphasises the need for pupils to record images and ideas from a variety of sources. There is a requirement for pupils to use a sketch-book and this is a particularly good, well tried method of recording thoughts, ideas and images. But a sketch-book is not just a drawing book and pupils should be encouraged to write their thoughts, to make colour notes, to use it as a scrapbook for newspaper and magazine clippings, their own photographs, train or theatre tickets etc., and to experiment with alternative drawing or mark-making materials. In some schools it may be possible for pupils to make their own personal sketch-books, on a large or small scale, using different kinds and colours of paper and creating their own designs for the covers.

Increasingly, there are other methods of recording visual information. At Key Stage Two, many pupils will have experience in the use of simple cameras and if they do not have their own, they may have access to one. Some time could be devoted to methods of using cameras, ranging from the fairly straightforward aspects of loading and unloading films, to the implication of different film speeds, composing and cropping images and creating composite images using a number of shots. Some schools have the use of video cameras and pupils can use these to explore and research visual ideas. Most classrooms now have their own computers and it is possible to record and print ideas, images and other information for use in sketch-books. Pupils can even keep a notebook on a computer disc.

Pupils experience visual material in a wide variety of different forms. Images are screened and presented in many contexts, to different purposes and in various ways. Pupils will become more visually literate and more conscious of the implications of such forms by discussing them and where possible, by using them in work of their own.

Materials and tools

The Programmes of Study associated with the end of the Key Stage Statements (c) for AT1 relating to the elements of art have specific practical implications as do the Scottish requirements, Using media. POS v expects pupils to explore different materials, tools and techniques. Primary schools vary greatly in the facilities which they can afford to offer their pupils, but there is an expectation here that the children will have the possibility of experiencing more than just the paper, pencils and paint that represents the bare minimum in many institutions. Some schools have teachers who may be specialists in particular areas such as pottery, jewellery or printmaking. Schools may wish these skills to be exploited and shared with the pupils and will back it up with materials and equipment. There are exciting 'draw and paint' software packages that can be acquired for the school computer and which may also be very useful in servicing other areas of the curriculum. There is a considerably wider range of materials and tools for making art nowadays and schools should try to reflect this in the experiences they offer children in art.

However, there are enormous differences in the nature and quality of even the basic traditional drawing materials. The school which simply has a tray of HB pencils is not going to be able to give pupils the experience of various thicknesses and grades of pencil lead. A big soft 6B graphite stick will give a deep velvety line quite different from the pale hard line made by a thin 2H pencil. On rough paper the marks will have a grainy effect, whereas on smooth paper there will be a more even distribution of tones. A coloured pencil will produce shading of a certain kind, whereas a coloured pastel, chalk or oil pastel quite another. If the coloured pencil is water-soluble, a drawing can be modified with a clean damp brush or the pencil can be used to draw on damp paper to give quite different effects.

If basic materials are to be bought, then teachers should be aware of these possibilities. The same is true of painting materials. For although schools may reasonably go for the cheapest option, buying powder colour and mixing this with water and a pva medium to produce a serviceable paint, it can also make sense to buy in a few good quality acrylic colours, for example, to give pupils experience of another kind of painting. If transparent techniques are used, very little paint is required and it will give the children good experience of colour mixing and painting in layers, for example. Four or five basic colours are all that is required as, for example: Phthalo (cyanine) Blue, Phthalo (cyanine) Green, Quinacridone Red, Azo Yellow, Burnt Sienna and Titanium White. From the red, yellow and blue in this basic set you can mix excellent secondary colours and a wide range of tertiaries.

Pupils can also only work to the level of their tools and it does seem to make sense for schools to acquire reasonable brushes, especially in the small round soft-hair range for the more careful work, where it is possible to buy relatively inexpensive synthetic hair brushes which come to a good point.

The POS here (AT1 POS v) makes the point that materials and tools are to be used experimentally. It is important to bear in mind that alongside work which introduces pupils to more traditional methods, is work that allows them to use the materials more freely and in different technical contexts. Traditional materials are constantly being re-evaluated and found new roles in art and so pupils should be encouraged to investigate new ways of working, including manipulating colour with less orthodox tools, for example, or painting on unusual supports such as plastic, stone or driftwood. The experimental aspect runs through the whole section of the Programme of Study (POS v-x) devoted to the elements of art and teachers should be constantly on the look-out for new ideas.

Working in context

The elements of art should not be considered out of context. There is some arbitrariness about the list which becomes more meaningful when they are seen as an integral part of a larger scheme, topic or unit of work. A series of line drawings might be created using different materials, pencil, charcoal or crayon, for example, as studies towards a larger work made by an individual or a group. One of the studies might be used as the basis for a string print in which the line drawing is re-created in string glued to stiff cardboard from which a print can be taken. Another might be used as the basis for a twig drawing, in which its outlines are re-created to a larger scale using twigs Blu-tacked to a wall.

These are just speculations, but the point is that notions of line are explored and discussed within a wider context than simply 'line' itself. This applies equally to the other 'elements' of art.

AT2 has at its core the knowledge and understanding of the context of art, craft and design within historical and contemporary cultures. This Attainment Target, which is meant to take up only half the time spent on AT1, should incorporate practical work, especially in its reference to pupils adopting and adapting the methods and approaches of other artists in their own work. Here the teacher has a particularly free hand in following personal enthusiasms since the pool from which ideas and techniques can be drawn is so vast.

Progression

One of the keys to a successful scheme of work in Art will be the building of progression into the activities. At this Key Stage, the children's capability in terms of practical work will develop perhaps more than at any other Key Stage. It is important for teachers to ensure therefore that children's achievements in this area – in terms of skills developed, materials, tools and techniques used – is assessed and records maintained so that the next year's work can build on this. A simple photocopiable record sheet is provided on page 149 for this purpose.

In the activity sections on the individual images that follow (Chapter 6) we have noted those practical activities which are more suitable in terms of skills or techniques required for older children. Also, there are differentiated tasks provided in many of the suggestions for thematic and cross curricular work in Chapter 5.

5. Planning Units of Work

In this chapter we outline two approaches to planning units of work in art: through art-focused units of work (what the 1993 NC document on planning for Key Stage Two terms 'blocked units of work') and through cross curricular approaches. Our intention in providing these units is to help teachers with planning and ensuring progression through the Key Stage.

Art-focused units of work

It can be difficult for teachers when faced with a seemingly arbitrary list of images to decide how these can be organised to help deliver the requirements of National Curriculum Art. It was the view of the Art Working Group – and this was re-iterated in the later Orders – that teaching should aim to bring together the various strands identified as being important, rather than working on them separately in isolation. In particular, it was considered extremely important not to separate the practice of art from its context, so we should aim to integrate AT1 and AT2 within a topic or unit of teaching. Similarly, the elements of art should be explored within a context in which they can be seen to function in a meaningful way. Although, in practice, a particular group of Programmes of Study might be given special focus at any one time, this would not be at the expense of all other areas of the art curriculum.

The selected images in *Approaches to Art* can be grouped in a number of ways that may be helpful to teachers when devising termly themes or topics in art. We have identified eight broad themes which could provide the basis for a term's work and listed the images that most closely relate to these themes. (In some cases, images used in one theme are also appropriate to others.) The themes are:

1. Images of Self and the Family
2. Telling a Story (Narrative)
3. Aspects of Landscape
4. Observing and Responding
5. Imagination and Invention
6. Transformations
7. Working in Three and Four Dimensions
8. Art for a Purpose (Applied Art, Craft and Design)

Each theme is described below, with an outline of how the theme could be developed to cover groups of POS items. This approach to planning reflects the recommendation on planning work in the Art non-Statutory Guidance (see D3, using related groups of POS items as a framework for planning), but we feel basing the work around an overall theme in addition to a selection of POS items will give it more coherence and a meaningful context.

19

The following images are appropriate to this theme. In each case, use the discussion ideas outlined in Chapter 6:

Picture 2 – Vuillard: 'Woman in Blue' (Moment of tenderness between mother and child)

Picture 4 – Gainsborough: 'Mr and Mrs Andrews' (Family couple in landscape setting)

Picture 13 – van Eyck: 'The Arnolfini Marriage' (Family couple, interior setting)

Picture 14 – Parmigianino: Self-portrait

Picture 18 – Efiaimbelo: 'Aloalo' (Memories of those we love who have died)

Picture 19 – Boccaccio's *De Claris Mulieribus* (Self-portrait)

Picture 20 – Vermeer: 'The Kitchenmaid' (Straight, non-idealised painting)

Picture 30 – Sargent: 'Carnation, Lily, Lily, Rose' (Focus on special moments in childhood)

Picture 31 – Woodrow: 'Twin Tub with Guitar' (Secret desires and longings)

Picture 38 – Sassetta: 'The Wish of the Young Saint Francis to become a Soldier' (Our ideals and aspirations)

Picture 40 – Lippi: 'Portrait of a Man and a Woman at a Casement' (Couple in interior setting)

Add to these self-portrait and relevant images from the other cultures, including drawing, painting, sculpture, photography, performance and film.

A unit of work, focusing on portraiture which resources particular areas of the Programme of Study, is outlined below. Teachers can select other appropriate activities, listed under the pictures for this theme, to plan additional or alternative units of work.

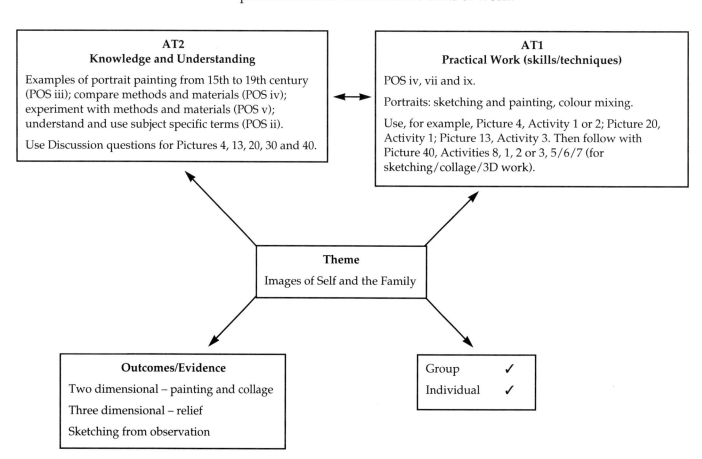

AT2
Knowledge and Understanding

Examples of portrait painting from 15th to 19th century (POS iii); compare methods and materials (POS iv); experiment with methods and materials (POS v); understand and use subject specific terms (POS ii).

Use Discussion questions for Pictures 4, 13, 20, 30 and 40.

AT1
Practical Work (skills/techniques)

POS iv, vii and ix.

Portraits: sketching and painting, colour mixing.

Use, for example, Picture 4, Activity 1 or 2; Picture 20, Activity 1; Picture 13, Activity 3. Then follow with Picture 40, Activities 8, 1, 2 or 3, 5/6/7 (for sketching/collage/3D work).

Theme
Images of Self and the Family

Outcomes/Evidence

Two dimensional – painting and collage

Three dimensional – relief

Sketching from observation

Group ✓
Individual ✓

The following images are particularly appropriate to this theme although many other images can be used in this way. In each case, use the discussion ideas outlined in Chapter 6:

Picture 3 – Bruegel: 'The Fall of Icarus'
Picture 6 – Frontispiece of the *Kuttenberg Kanzional*
Picture 8 – Martin: 'The Bard'
Picture 9 – 'Baz Bahadur and Rupmati'
Picture 24 – Lorraine: 'Seaport with the Embarkation of Saint Ursula'
Picture 32 – Miró: 'The Red Sun'
Picture 38 – Sassetta: 'The wish of the Young Saint Francis to become a Soldier'

One unit of work based around this theme is outlined below. Teachers can select other appropriate activities from those listed under any of the pictures grouped under this theme. Cross refer also to page 31, Links with English.

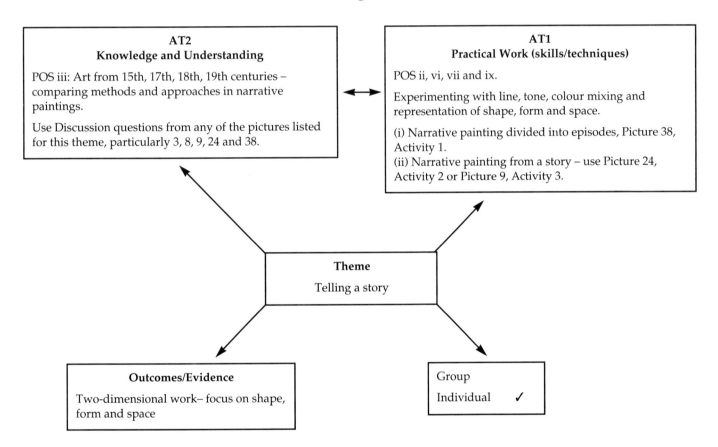

AT2
Knowledge and Understanding

POS iii: Art from 15th, 17th, 18th, 19th centuries – comparing methods and approaches in narrative paintings.

Use Discussion questions from any of the pictures listed for this theme, particularly 3, 8, 9, 24 and 38.

AT1
Practical Work (skills/techniques)

POS ii, vi, vii and ix.

Experimenting with line, tone, colour mixing and representation of shape, form and space.

(i) Narrative painting divided into episodes, Picture 38, Activity 1.
(ii) Narrative painting from a story – use Picture 24, Activity 2 or Picture 9, Activity 3.

Theme
Telling a story

Outcomes/Evidence

Two-dimensional work– focus on shape, form and space

Group
Individual   ✓

The following images are appropriate to this theme. In each case, use the discussion ideas outlined in Chapter 6:

Picture 3 – Bruegel: 'The Fall of Icarus'
Picture 4 – Gainsborough: 'Mr and Mrs Andrews'
Picture 7 – Moore: 'King and Queen'
Picture 9 – 'Baz Bahadur and Rupmati'
Picture 16 and 17 – Constable: 'Cloud Studies'
Picture 23 – Friedrich: 'Two Men Contemplating the Moon'
Picture 25 – Morisot: 'Summer's Day'
Picture 26 – Hokusai: 'Wild Sea at Chōshi'
Picture 37 – Gilbert and George: 'Weather Window'

Work on two aspects of this theme is planned out below focusing on different elements of the Programme of Study. Teachers could add further or alternative units related to this theme using some of the activities listed for the above images.

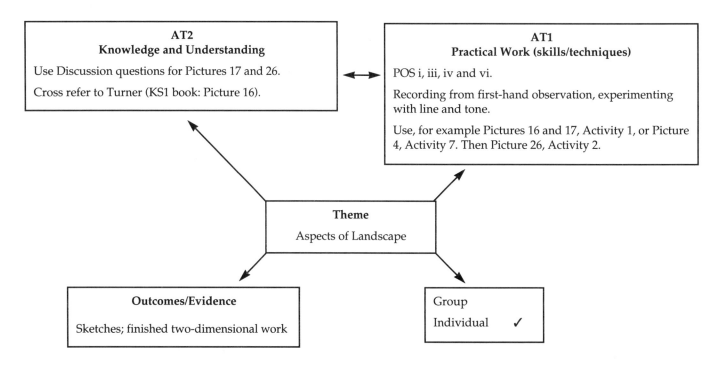

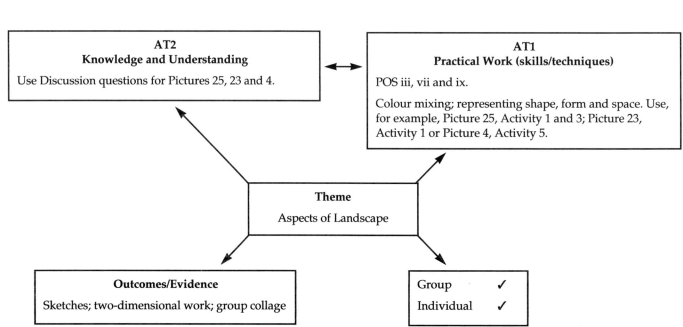

The following images are appropriate to this theme. In each case, use the discussion ideas outlined in Chapter 6:

Picture 2 – Vuillard: 'Woman in Blue'
Picture 4 – Gainsborough: 'Mr and Mrs Andrews'
Picture 11 – Arikha: 'Scarlet Scarf on a Studio Chair'
Picture 12 – Palissy: 'Oval dish'
Picture 13 – van Eyck: 'The Arnolfini Marriage'
Pictures 16 and 17 – Constable: 'Cloud Studies'
Picture 19 – Boccaccio's *De Claris Mulieribus*
Picture 25 – Morisot: 'Summer's Day'
Picture 29 – Delacroix: 'Interior of Moroccan House'
Picture 30 – Sargent: 'Carnation, Lily, Lily, Rose'
Picture 31 – Woodrow: 'Twin Tub with Guitar'
Picture 34 – Cézanne: 'Pommes Vertes'

Two projects based around the theme of Observing and Responding are outlined below. Teachers can select further activities listed for the above images in Chapter 6 to plan additional or alternative units of work based on this theme.

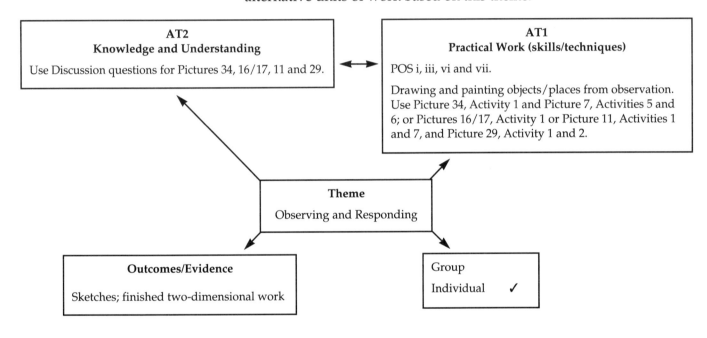

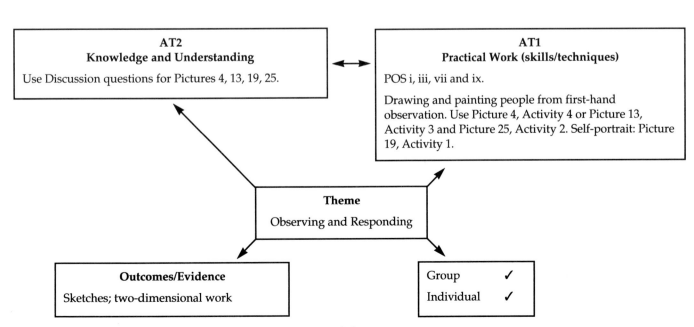

23

The following images are appropriate to this theme. In each case, use the discussion ideas outlined in Chapter 6:

Picture 8 – Martin : 'The Bard'
Picture 22 – Blake: 'The Tyger'
Picture 23 – Friedrich: 'Two Men Contemplating the Moon'
Picture 32 – Miró: 'The Red Sun'
Picture 36 – Linares: 'Crab/Frog'

A unit of work based around this theme is outlined below. Teachers can select other appropriate activities listed under the pictures for this theme, to plan further units of work. One approach might be to link art work on this theme with imaginative writing – see page 32.

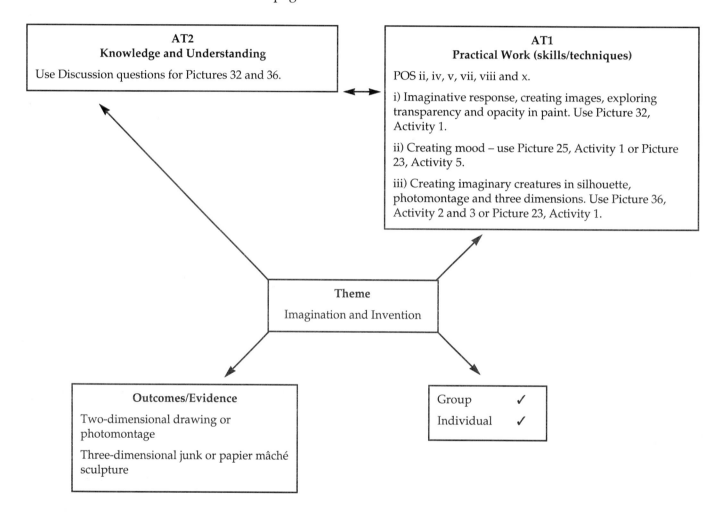

AT2
Knowledge and Understanding

Use Discussion questions for Pictures 32 and 36.

AT1
Practical Work (skills/techniques)

POS ii, iv, v, vii, viii and x.

i) Imaginative response, creating images, exploring transparency and opacity in paint. Use Picture 32, Activity 1.

ii) Creating mood – use Picture 25, Activity 1 or Picture 23, Activity 5.

iii) Creating imaginary creatures in silhouette, photomontage and three dimensions. Use Picture 36, Activity 2 and 3 or Picture 23, Activity 1.

Theme
Imagination and Invention

Outcomes/Evidence

Two-dimensional drawing or photomontage

Three-dimensional junk or papier mâché sculpture

Group   ✓
Individual   ✓

The following images are appropriate to this theme. In each case, use the discussion ideas outlined in Chapter 6:
Pictures 14/15 – Parmigianino and Scrots portraits
Picture 31 – Woodrow: 'Twin Tub with Guitar'
Picture 36 – Linares: 'Crab/Frog'
Picture 37 – Gilbert and George: 'Weather Window'

Two units of work based around the theme of Transformations are outlined below. Teachers can select other appropriate activities from those listed under the images above in Chapter 6, to plan additional or alternative units of work.

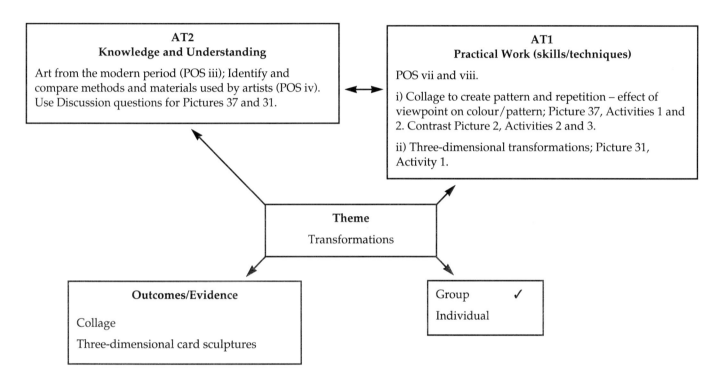

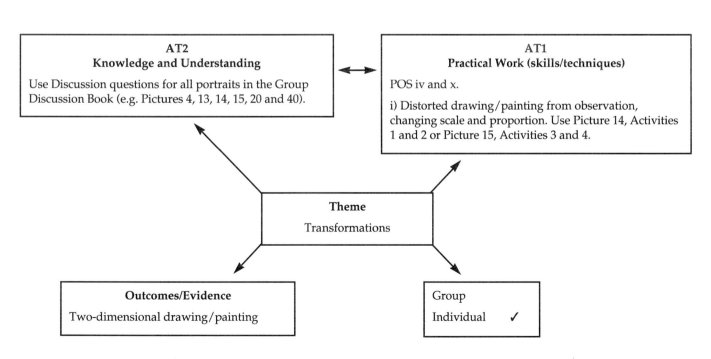

The following images are appropriate to this theme. Use the discussion ideas outlined in Chapter 6 to talk about aspects of three-dimensional work.

Picture 1 – Silver-gilt casket
Picture 6 – 'Dancing Hora'
Picture 7 – Moore: 'King and Queen'
Picture 12 – Palissy: 'Oval dish
Picture 18 – Efiaimbelo: 'Aloalo'
Picture 21 – Jiminez: 'Wood Animals'
Picture 27 – Gold attachments
Picture 31 – Woodrow: 'Twin Tub and Guitar'
Picture 35 – Lewis Chessmen
Picture 36 – Linares: 'Crab/Frog'

Projects focusing on small-scale and larger-scale three-dimensional work are outlined below. Teachers can use any of the activities listed for the above images to plan units of work in three dimensions.

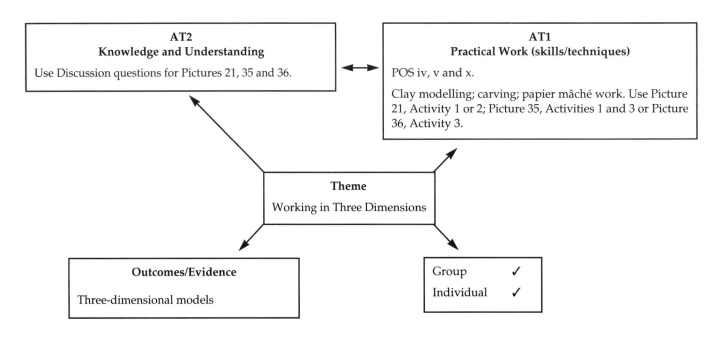

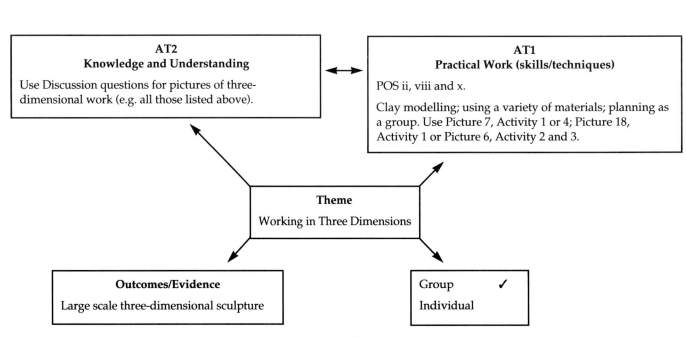

The following images are appropriate to this unit. In each case, use the discussion ideas outlined in Chapter 6:

Picture 1 –   Silver-gilt casket
Picture 10 – Bronze aquamanile
Picture 12 – Palissy: 'Oval dish'
Picture 13 – van Eyck: 'The Arnolfini Marriage'
Picture 18 – Efiaimbelo: 'Aloalo'
Picture 27 – Persian Gold Attachments
Picture 28 – Morris: 'Acanthus and Vine'
Picture 35 – Lewis Chessmen

One unit of work based on the theme Art for a Purpose is outlined below. Teachers can use any of the activities listed for the above pictures in Chapter 6 to create further units of work around this theme.

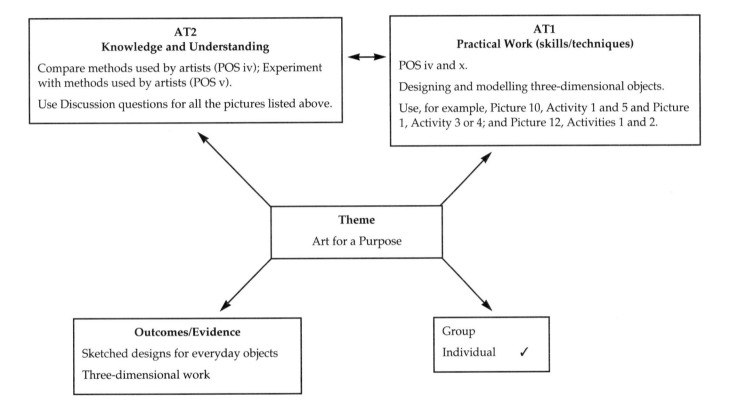

AT2
Knowledge and Understanding

Compare methods used by artists (POS iv); Experiment with methods used by artists (POS v).

Use Discussion questions for all the pictures listed above.

AT1
Practical Work (skills/techniques)

POS iv and x.

Designing and modelling three-dimensional objects.

Use, for example, Picture 10, Activity 1 and 5 and Picture 1, Activity 3 or 4; and Picture 12, Activities 1 and 2.

Theme
Art for a Purpose

Outcomes/Evidence

Sketched designs for everyday objects

Three-dimensional work

Group
Individual   ✓

Cross curricular approaches

Although *Approaches to Art* is closely linked with the Art in the National Curriculum documents, the study of art works can be integrated into most other subjects in the curriculum and we strongly advocate this approach. Indeed, to separate art from other subjects leads to the mystification of art which is to be avoided. Art need not be baffling – something which can only be enjoyed or 'appreciated' by a small body of privileged initiated people – and the more that it becomes part of the daily life of our pupils, the more confident and secure they feel with it, the more they will accept it and feel able to enjoy it in the future.

The following cross curricular links are only suggestions – starting points if you like – of a process which is almost limitless. We hope that teachers will use and develop ideas outlined below for the enrichment of their class teaching.

In the next part of this chapter we will be looking at various subjects and suggesting ways for making links to those subjects using both the Group Discussion Book which goes with this Teachers' Resource Book, but also mentioning the book for Years 1-3 (which we refer to here as the KS1 book) as we realise that many schools will have both. For those schools that organise some of their work thematically (i.e. around topics that include several areas of the curriculum) many of the links suggested below can be used. For example, see under Science for topics such as Water, Weather, Colour and Light. For Ourselves, look back to the art-focused topic (on page 20) for work on portrait and self-portrait. For Transport/Journeys, Food and Farming see under History.

History

It is often helpful to look at artefacts which people from long ago have left behind. The notion that art lasts longer than people is an intriguing one for children of junior age and it is an idea which may not really have occurred to them.

Paintings (including such things as manuscript illuminations) can be invaluable in showing how people used to live and also giving a 'feel' for a period through clothes and so on (see Hi AT1, describing and explaining historical change). For example, Picture 20, Vermeer's 'Kitchenmaid', although painted in Holland in the 17th century can give quite a vivid idea of domestic life in Europe at the time of the Stuarts and could lead to a comparison with then and now in terms of kitchen design and equipment, food, clothes and so on. Books of recipes survive from this period . . . what might she be cooking? How?

Teachers should be aware, however, that artists through the ages have painted themes taken from previous centuries. For example, in 16th and 17th-century Europe it was fashionable to paint stories from the Ancient Greek and Roman myths. We do quite often use these mythological paintings at the National Gallery to bring these traditional tales to life.

In the 19th century, in particular, some artists painted scenes from history many of which are totally inaccurate in historical terms. For example, 'The Execution of Lady Jane Grey' (an event which took place in the 16th century) was the subject of a very famous melodramatic 19th-century painting by the French artist, Delaroche. We do not recommend using this type of picture to teach Tudor history, and in order not to cause confusion, we have not included any pictures of this sort in the Group Discussion Books.

In addition to paintings, sculptures and pieces of decorative art are very useful for enriching history teaching. (See page 38 for a chart including a description and date of all the images in the KS2 Group Discussion Book.) Not only can they give rise to interesting discussion about what we can and cannot learn from these sources, but can also lead to discussion about what the object was for, who would have owned it and how it has survived the centuries and so on. Finding artefacts from the past is not just the province of special people. It can happen to anyone – and does. This idea can be very exciting and children in some circumstances can be encouraged to discover things themselves. For example, if the children live (as many do) in a place which has been inhabited for more than 100 years and if they have a garden, they will find bits of broken crockery and clay pipes, just lying around. This is archaeology at a basic level and exactly how many art 'finds' are made. In towns, holes in the road dug by electricity or telephone engineers will also yield finds, such as oyster shells and crockery. This is the way that jewellery and many coins are discovered.

Visual material of all sorts enriches the teaching of history and makes it seem more relevant and 'real'. One of the requirements of the Programme of Study is that pupils should learn about the past from a range of historical sources including artefacts; pictures and photographs; documents and printed sources. Attainment Target 3, the use of historical sources, focuses on acquiring evidence from a variety of sources and many of the images in the KS1 and KS2 books will augment those in pupils' history books. The Discussion questions will help introduce a general discussion of the picture from which the teacher can lead to a discussion of the picture from a specifically historical perspective.

Many of the Discussion questions provided will also help pupils start to develop the required variety of perspectives (particularly social, religious, cultural and aesthetic) in the study of history. We give you some ideas below for images in the Group Discussion Books which tie in with the Core study units in KS2 History.

Invaders and Settlers
KS1 book: Picture 21, Viking bracelet; Pictures 11 and 41, Roman Mosaics. KS2 book: Picture 35, Viking Chessmen. Tell the story of their discovery. Look at where they were found on a map. How did these chessmen come to be there? What routes were the Vikings using? Where were they going?

Tudors
KS1 book: Picture 49, Tudor picture book – what was the purpose of a book like this and what are the objects beneath the flower illustrations? Picture 15, *Da Costa Book of Hours* – for a domestic interior of c.1515. Picture 33, Oliver – miniatures – for the clothes.

KS2 book: Picture 15, Scrots's 'Portrait of Edward VI'. Picture 3, Bruegel's 'Fall of Icarus', shows ploughing in the 16th century and also a ship.

Stuarts
KS1 book: Pictures which were painted in Europe in the 17th century are 25, Avercamp's 'A Winter Scene' and 34, Velazquez's 'The Infant Philip Prosper'.

KS2 book: Picture 20, Vermeer's 'Kitchenmaid'; Picture 24, Lorraine's 'Embarkation' – although a History painting, it is set in 'modern' i.e. 17th-century times – showing ships of the period, and also the interest in classical architecture at this period; Picture 33, Guercino's 'Aurora' shows interest at this time in classical mythology.

Victorian Britain

KS1 book: Picture 51, Dyce's 'Pegwell Bay'. The invention of the railway led to the development of seaside holiday resorts. Interest in science at this time is evident – the people are collecting fossils. Notice the carefully painted geology and the comet in the sky. Talk about the clothes.

KS2 book: Picture 28, Morris's 'Acanthus and Vine' tapestry. This was made partly as a reaction against manufactured goods, such as those displayed at the Great Exhibition of 1851. Relate it also to the beginning of the Arts and Crafts Movement. Picture 30, Sargent's 'Carnation, Lily, Lily, Rose' – for the clothes.

Ancient Greece

KS2 book: Picture 6, 'Dancing Hora'; Picture 3, Bruegel's 'The Fall of Icarus'. The story, while barely illustrated here, is captivating and can be tied in with the story of Theseus and the Minotaur.

Exploration and Encounters 1450-1550

Travel and trade in the 15th and 16th centuries was extensive. KS1 book: Picture 13, van Eyck's 'The Arnolfini Marriage' shows an Italian merchant who lived in Bruges, for example. There is evidence of trade in many art works – such as the use of the blue pigment, ultramarine, which (before the 19th century) came only from Afghanistan.

Until the 19th century, with the discovery of rubber (for tyres), the invention of tarmac (for smooth roads) and the development of the railways (for quick, easy and relatively cheap public transport), moving from place to place was difficult, dangerous and uncomfortable and did not change much from century to century. Pictures in the KS2 book such as 3, 8, 24, 38 could be used in a discussion (and also KS1 book: Picture 24).

Some of the pictures in both the Key Stage One and Two Group Discussion Books can also be used to resource some of the thematic history supplementary units:

Writing and printing

KS2 book:	Picture 5	*Kuttenberg Kanzional*
	Picture 22	Blake's 'The Tyger'
	Picture 26	Hokusai's 'Wild Sea at Chōshi'
	Picture 39	*Luttrell Psalter*
KS1 book:	Picture 15	*Da Costa Book of Hours*
	Picture 37	Ravilious's engraving
	Picture 49	Tudor picture book

Domestic Life, Families and Childhood

KS2 book:	Picture 4	Gainsborough's 'Mr and Mrs Andrews'
	Picture 13	van Eyck's 'The Arnolfini Marriage'
	Picture 20	Vermeer's 'The Kitchenmaid'
	Picture 30	Sargent's 'Carnation, Lily, Lily, Rose'
	Picture 40	Lippi's 'Portrait of a Man and a Woman'

KS1 book: Picture 15   *Da Costa Book of Hours*
              Pictures 21-23   Jewellery
              Pictures 28-29   Candlestick/pottery
              Picture 33   Oliver's 'Miniature'
              Picture 34   Velazquez's 'The Infant Philip Prosper'
              Picture 46   Devis's 'Family group'

Ships and Seafaring
KS2 book: Picture 3   Bruegel's 'The Fall of Icarus'
              Picture 24   Lorraine's 'Seaport'

English

AT1 Speaking and listening
Inviting children to talk about a work of art is an excellent way of
encouraging dialogue and developing vocabulary. Any picture in the
Group Discussion Book lends itself to this. All we suggest is that the
teacher prepares a number of new words to introduce during these
discussions – the words as suggested by pupils or teacher being
written on the blackboard as the discussion progresses.

There are various games you can play with prints or postcards.
For example, choose an image and work out the words which describe
it best. For example KS2 book: Picture 23, Friedrich's 'Two Men', you
might choose: 'eerie', 'spooky', 'dark', 'thoughtful', and so on. The rest
of the group have to guess which image is being referred to from the
words used. This could lead on to some imaginative writing.

AT2 Reading
Pictures have stories to tell – working out a painting's story is a bit like
reading. Sometimes a narrative is illustrated (e.g. KS2 book: Picture 3,
Bruegel's 'The Fall of Icarus'; Picture 8, Martin's 'The Bard'; Picture 24,
Lorraine's 'Seaport'; and Picture 38, Sassetta's 'The Wish of the Young
Saint Francis'.

Sometimes the story a picture has to tell is more subtle than that, or
even ambiguous (e.g. KS2 book: Picture 13, van Eyck's 'The Arnolfini
Marriage'; Picture 40, Lippi's 'Portrait of a Man and a Woman'). Story
telling in words or pictures involves a process of selection. What the
narrator (or painter) chooses to include and what to leave out are both
of great importance.

Try getting the children to tell the story of a painting which has
a clearly defined narrative – to develop the child's ability to re-tell
someone else's story. Then ask them to make up a story about another
type of image, such as KS2 book: Picture 41, Ayres's 'Chanticlear';
Picture 1, the silver-gilt casket, as an exercise to develop imagination
and fantasy.

AT3 Writing
Some artists have incorporated words and images on a single page.
This is something this age-group like to do and can form the focus
of an English and art topic. Refer to KS2 book: Picture 22, Blake's
'The Tyger' – where the artist made up and wrote out the poem and
illustrated the page himself. More able top junior children will be able
to do this and we suggest taking this in several stages – perfect the
poem before attempting the illuminated page. (See Activity 1.)

Look also at the activities on p 140, KS2 book: Picture 39, *Luttrell Psalter*. Here the words in Latin are not the artist's own. We suggest the use of short sayings for illustration might be suitable here e.g. 'a fool and his money are soon parted'. See also Picture 1 for work on mottos and proverbs.

We also suggest with top juniors that some attention is paid to handwriting and calligraphy. Once some skill in writing is achieved, children of this age will enjoy trying out new styles. Encourage them to develop their own personal signature. (Look at KS2 book: Picture 13, van Eyck's 'The Arnolfini Marriage' for a really splendid example.)

Imaginative writing

Many of the images in the Group Discussion Books could provide a stimulus for imaginative writing, either based on the theme or mood of the work itself or from the child's own imagination in response to the image.

The following images could be particularly appropriate for story writing based on a picture: KS2 book: Picture 3, Bruegel's 'The Fall of Icarus'; Picture 9, 'Baz Bahadur and Rupmati' (Activities 3 and 4); Picture 8, Martin's 'The Bard'; Picture 11, Arikha's 'Scarlet Scarf' (Activity 9) and Picture 38, Sassetta's 'Wish of the Young Saint Francis'. KS1 book: Picture 4, Uccello's 'Saint George and the Dragon'; Picture 24, Patenier's 'Saint Jerome in a Rocky Landscape'.

The following images may be appropriate as starting points for imaginative writing with a focus on mood or atmosphere: KS2 book: Picture 22, Blake's 'The Tyger'; Picture 23, Friedrich's 'Two Men Contemplating the Moon'; Picture 25, Morisot's 'Summer's Day'. KS1 book: Picture 51, Dyce's 'Pegwell Bay'.

Geography

Art and geography may at first glance not seem to go naturally together; however there are quite a number of useful links which can be made. Perhaps the most obvious and the least interesting is the idea of marking on a map where a particular art work, or artist came from – we don't really recommend this.

Pictorial images can be used for children to describe what they can see in geographical terms – for the development of geographical vocabulary. For example, KS2 book: Picture 3, Bruegel's 'The Fall of Icarus'; Picture 5, the *Kuttenberg Kanzional* and Picture 8, Martin's 'The Bard'. KS1 book: Picture 51, Dyce's 'Pegwell Bay'. They can also attempt to make a map of a place shown in a picture (KS2 book: Picture 3, Bruegel's 'The Fall of Icarus' and Picture 8, Martin's 'The Bard').

The concept of drawing a plan can be reinforced by asking children to make a ground plan of a painting, such as KS2 book: Picture 13, van Eyck's 'The Arnolfini Marriage' or even just the objects on a table, KS2 book: Picture 20 Vermeer's 'The Kitchenmaid'. This linking of still life to plan drawing can be developed in the following way. Make a collection of objects e.g. mug, plate, salt cellar, jug, on a table. Arrange them, and ask the children to draw the shapes they make on the table.

By superimposing letter/number co-ordinates on an image the children can be taught to use them. Ask 'what is in square B7?' for example. This kind of activity can be turned into a game.

Fieldwork

Fieldwork is part of the study of the local area in Geography and can be fruitfully linked with work in art. Working from first-hand observation is a requirement of the art curriculum and several of the activities included in the Group Discussion Book would link well with the Geography curriculum, particularly AT1, Geographical Skills and AT2, Knowledge and Understanding of places. For example, KS2 book: Picture 4, Gainsborough's 'Mr and Mrs Andrews'; Picture 16 and 17, Constable's 'Cloud Studies'.

Weather

Sun KS2 book: Picture 3, Bruegel's 'The Fall of Icarus'; Picture 25, Morisot's 'Summer's Day'; Picture 29, Delacroix's 'Interior of a Moroccan House'. KS1 book: Picture 16, Turner's 'Sunset, Tours'.
Mist KS2 book: Picture 9, 'Baz Bahadur and Rupmati'.
Clouds KS2 book: Pictures 16 and 17 for cloud studies – children can be taken out to draw and paint clouds and to make the kinds of observations on their work which Constable did.
Wind KS2 book: Picture 18, Efiaimbelo's 'Aloalo'; Picture 26, Hokusai's 'Wild Sea at Chōshi'. KS1 book: Picture 4, Uccello's 'Saint George and the Dragon'.
Rain KS1 book: Picture 5, Rousseau's 'Tropical Storm with a Tiger'.
Frost KS1 book: Picture 25, Avercamp's 'A Winter Scene'.

Seasons

Winter KS1 book: Picture 15, *Da Costa Book of Hours*; Picture 25, Avercamp's 'A Winter Scene'.
Spring KS1 book: Picture 47, Botticelli's 'Primavera'.
Summer KS1 book: Pictures 35 and 36, van Gogh's 'Sunflowers'; Picture 48, van Os's 'Fruit and Flowers'; Picture 52, Rego's 'On the Beach'. KS2 book: Picture 4, Gainsborough's 'Mr and Mrs Andrews'; Picture 25, Morisot's 'Summer's Day'; Picture 30, Sargent's 'Carnation, Lily, Lily, Rose'.
Autumn KS1 book: Picture 17, Goldsworthy's 'Maple Patch'; Picture 51, Dyce's 'Pegwell Bay'. KS2 book: Picture 39, the *Luttrell Psalter*.

Water (selective list)

KS1 book: Picture 5 (Rousseau – rain/rain forest); Picture 19 (Ninevah: reed beds); Picture 25 (Avercamp – floods and frost); Picture 26 (Egyptian – river Nile and garden with pool); Picture 46 (Devis – artificial lake/canal in garden); Picture 51 (Dyce – English coastline). KS2 book: Picture 3 (Bruegel – sea/shoreline); Picture 8 (Martin – rushing torrents in mountains); Pictures 16 and 17 (Constable – rain-clouds); Picture 24 (Lorraine – seaport); Picture 26 (Hokusai – wild sea); Picture 27 (Oxus – treasure found in river bank).

Geology

The notion of a cross-section of land can be tied in with the *Kuttenberg Kanzional* (although the picture is fanciful) and of course the idea of mining for metal ores. Some materials used for paint-making are mined, such as lapis lazuli – to make ultramarine (blue), cinnabar to make natural vermilion (red), azurite (blue) and malachite (green). KS1 book: Picture 51, Dyce's 'Pegwell Bay' shows geological rock formations.

Classification

Art historians classify art objects just as scientists classify animals and plants. These are really sorting systems. How do we sort out works of art? How do museums and galleries sort them? Size? Subject matter? Age? Materials used for construction? Country of origin? Using a collection of a wide range of postcards of works of art, you could construct a 'museum director' game and work out a system of display. Art galleries usually sort paintings and sculptures according to when they were made and where. Although in larger museums, *where* may take precedence over *when*. So, for example, you may find all the Chinese art separated entirely from the European art.

When visiting museums (both science and art) and galleries, it is a good idea for children to understand what classification systems are in operation.

History of science

Changes in belief and knowledge in, for example, astronomy: Aurora the goddess of the dawn sets out before the sun and drives her chariot across the sky (KS2 book: Picture 33, Guercino's 'Aurora'). Also connected with astronomy is Friedrich's 'Two Men Contemplating the Moon' (KS2 book: Picture 23), and KS1 book: Picture 51, Dyce's 'Pegwell Bay' – which contains Donati's Comet.

Light (Sc AT4)

Children can be encouraged to observe that some colours reflect light better than others. Artists in the past have noticed and exploited this to get certain effects in their pictures. (KS2 book: Picture 30, Sargent's 'Carnation, Lily, Lily, Rose'). An important figure in a painting is often given a light or a bright colour to make him or her stand out. (For example, KS2 book: Picture 8, Martin's 'The Bard'.)

Note, the use of gold in paintings made to go on church altars would have reflected the flickering candlelight. This effect is hard to imagine and printed reproductions are very inadequate for this purpose. We have not included an example of this type of picture in the KS2 Discussion book and only Picture 44 in the KS1 book, by the Master of the Saint Bartholomew altarpiece, comes anywhere near.

How we use light in our homes can also be discussed. For example, candles – KS2 book: Picture 13, van Eyck's 'The Arnolfini Marriage'; Picture 30, Sargent's 'Carnation, Lily, Lily, Rose'. KS1 book: Picture 15, *Da Costa Book of Hours* (this also shows cooking over an open fire); Picture 28, brass candlestick.

Reflected light is another topic which can be studied. For example, convex mirrors – in van Eyck's 'The Arnolfini Marriage' (KS2 book: Picture 13) and one was used to paint the Parmigianino's 'Self-Portrait' (KS2 book: Picture 14); the use of a flat mirror for a self-portrait in the illustration for *De Claris Mulieribus* (KS2 book: Picture 19); shiny silver bowl to be seen in Chardin's 'The Silver Goblet' (KS1 book: Picture 1) and interesting, if subtle, shine on the surface of the pots etc. in Vermeer's, 'The Kitchenmaid' (KS2 book: Picture 20). Look at the reflections in water in Turner's 'Sunset, Tours' (KS1 book: Picture 16) and Devis's 'Family Group in a Garden' (KS1 book: Picture 46) and Lorraine's 'Seaport' (KS2 book: Picture 24).

Colour

Colour and light are topics which are often usefully studied together. Mixing coloured pigments and mixing coloured light are two different things – creating different results. Colour pigment-mixing comes within the scope of this book and children at junior age should be made familiar with primary and secondary paint colours. (See Picture 30 page 116.)

There are also differences between pigments and dyes. A pigment can sometimes be made from a dye, but a chemical process is involved. We refer to dyeing in connection with the William Morris tapestry (KS2 book: Picture 28). Making colour before the industrial revolution was usually done by the artist him or herself from natural materials such as minerals, earths and extracts from animal and plant stuffs. For information about manufactured pigments which could be bought in tubes see page 102.

Many museums and galleries employ scientists to tell the curators what the objects they are looking after are made of, and to monitor the conditions in which they are kept. They analyse, for example, the air in a museum for noxious gases, and they calculate how much light can be allowed to fall on an exhibit without damage being caused. They monitor room temperature, humidity and so on.

Additionally, many museums and galleries employ restorers who repair and clean old works of art. While Key Stage Two children do not need to go into this sort of thing in detail, it is a good idea for them to be aware that these people exist.

Mathematics

Mathematics is about shape, number, proportion, pattern, symmetry, size, area and volume . . . and so is art! There are all sorts of ways of making cross curricular links here – all it takes is a bit of imagination. Rather than listing all the possible individual items here we are just offering a few ideas.

Perspective

When artists want to create an illusion of space on a flat surface they sometimes use linear perspective – a concept which was first worked out mathematically in Italy in the 15th century, but which had been used to a limited extent empirically before that. In its simplest form, all the lines in a picture converge towards a single vanishing point. Things in the foreground are larger than those in the background and their reduction in size happens at a fixed and logical rate.

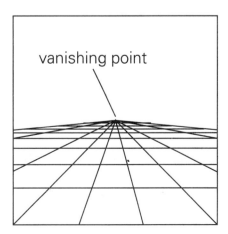
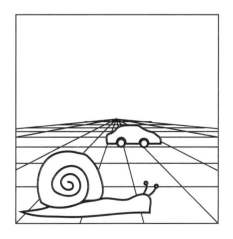

The golden section

This is a 19th-century name given to a system of proportion described in Euclid which was much used by European artists from the 15th century on. It was known as the 'divine proportion'. It is more economical in its terms than any other proportion. In its simplest form it is this – Line AB is cut at point C. The position of C is determined by this proportion: AC is to CB what CB is to AB.

In practical terms, point C is about a third of the way between A and B. Artists often use this proportion (knowingly) in the composition of their paintings – so, for example, the position of the horizon in Lorraine's 'Seaport' (KS2 book: Picture 24) looks as if it may have been calculated according to this principle. Bright top juniors should be able to grasp this idea.

AC:CB::CB:AB and AB = AC + CB

Pattern and symmetry

Look at KS2 book: Picture 1, Silver-gilt casket; Picture 19, Boccaccio's *De Claris Mulieribus*; Picture 22, Blake's 'The Tyger'; Picture 28, Morris's 'Acanthus and Vine' tapestry; Picture 37, Gilbert and George's 'Weather Window'. KS1 book: Picture 12, Long's 'Mud Hand Circle'; Picture 18, Matisse's 'La Gerbe'; Picture 19, Stone relief; Picture 23, Gold pendant; Picture 42, Turkish tile panel.

Measures

Calculate how old an art work is. Calculate how many tesserae/tiles have been used to make an image. KS1 book: Picture 41, Roman mosaic; Picture 42, Turkish tile panel. KS2 book: Picture 37, Gilbert and George's 'Weather Window'.

Calculate the approximate size of a room which shows a tiled floor. KS2 book: Picture 19, Boccaccio's *De Claris Mulieribus*.

The measurement of time can be discussed in connection with the idea of a candle clock in van Eyck's 'The Arnolfini Marriage' (KS2 book: Picture 13).

Technology

While the curriculum in Technology is still under review it is difficult to make too precise a linkage between work in art and technology. However, there is a very close relationship between many aspects of the practical activities suggested here for art and the type of activity children will be undertaking in technology-focused work.

Planning, designing and making are all activities central to technology and are key also to much practical work in art. The suggestions for three-dimensional units of work in this book, for example, can be used as a focus for coverage of both the art and technology curricula.

Progression and assessment

Although there are currently no statutory requirements laid upon teachers to assess children formally at the end of Key Stage Two, it is clearly helpful to have some means of building progression into children's work year by year. By recording the work children have covered each year, the next year can build upon these achievements. The photocopiable record sheet on page 149 is designed for this purpose. There is space for recording information about three projects which will probably be enough for assessing progress against the key criteria for each year. Alongside this record, if at all possible, it is a good idea to build a cumulative but selective portfolio of each child's work as they progress through the junior school.

Progression should be built into each year's scheme of work in two areas:

a) **knowledge and understanding**
Discussion of works of art should be in a widening context (and not just concentrate on the picture itself). Children's use of language and knowledge of special vocabulary when talking about pictures should be developed carefully year by year.

b) **practical work**
There are several areas in which pupils' progress can be assessed and built upon:
i)   How good are they at developing ideas and seeing them through to finished work?
ii)   How is their knowledge and control of materials and techniques developing? Can they select appropriate materials and tools for a chosen task?
iii)   What progress do they show in their handling of key elements of art, e.g. colour, shape, space, line, tone?
iv)   Can they work well as part of a group?
v)   Is the context in which the child is working more challenging than that of last year's work?
vi)   Do they show a growing tendency to review and modify their work?
Recording comments in the above areas will help build a profile of the child's progress through the Key Stage.

Summary of pictures

Picture	Nationality of artist	Date	Material
1	English or French	c.1300	silver-gilt
2	French	c.1899	oil on cardboard
3	Flemish	c.1558	oil on canvas
4	English	c.1750	oil on canvas
5	Bavarian	c.1490	tempera on parchment
6	Greek	c.1st century B.C.	stone
7	English	1952-3	bronze
8	English	c.1817	oil on canvas
9	Indian	c.1720	gouache on paper
10	Germanic	15th century	bronze
11	Israeli	1989	oil on canvas
12	French	1560	glazed earthenware
13	Flemish	1434	oil on wood
14	Italian	1523-4	painted wooden roundel
15	Netherlandish	1546	painted wooden panel
16	English	1821	oil on paper
17	English	1821	oil on paper
18	African	1991-2	wood and acrylic
19	French	1402	illuminated manuscript
20	Dutch	1658	oil on canvas
21	Mexican	1960	paint on wood
22	English	1794	relief etching
23	German	1819-20	oil on canvas
24	French	1641	oil on canvas
25	French	1879	oil on canvas
26	Japanese	c.1832-3	coloured wood engraving
27	Persian	c.6th-3rd century B.C.	gold
28	English	c.1879	tapestry
29	French	1832	watercolour and pencil on paper
30	American	1885-6	oil on canvas
31	English	1981	washing machine
32	Spanish	1948	oil on canvas
33	Italian	1621-3	fresco and tempera
34	French	1873	oil on canvas
35	Scandinavian	12th century	ivory
36	Mexican	1989	paint and papier mâché
37	English	1989	postcards
38	Italian	1437-1444	egg tempera on wood
39	English	c.1340	illuminated manuscript
40	Italian	c.1440	tempera on wood
41	English	1988-9	oil on canvas

6. Resources and activities

Introduction

This chapter includes background information, suggested topics for discussion and practical activities related to each of the pictures in the Group Discussion Book.

The shaded box at the beginning of each section provides reference to the specific areas of the Programme of Study that the discussion topics and practical activities cover. Note that *the references are only to parts of the Programme of Study for Attainment Target 1 –* Investigating and Making – where specific activities can be used to cover specific areas of the AT, e.g. 'experiment with different qualities of line and tone', or 'plan and make three-dimensional structures'.

Two parts of AT1 (POS xi and xii) and all AT2 – Knowledge and Understanding – are not specifically referenced. This is intentional. Through discussing a range of the pictures in the Group Discussion Book and by carrying out related practical activities, children will cover the requirements of the whole of AT2 and AT1, POS xi and xii. For example, in our discussion and background information sections we ensure that subject specific terms are introduced as appropriate (see AT2, POS ii, 'Understand and use subject specific terms such as landscape, still life, mural' and we give guidance for developing specialist vocabulary (see AT1, POS xii, 'Use a developing specialist vocabulary to describe their work') through the discussion and background information sections.

Our collection of pictures covers a wide timespan and includes work by a carefully selected range of artists so that AT2 POS ii, 'Look at and discuss art from early, Renaissance and later periods in order to start to understand the way in which art was developed and the contribution of influential artists or groups of artists to that development' can begin to be met.

We have also not referenced AT1, POS xi 'adapt or modify their work in order to realise their ideas and explain and justify the changes they have made' specifically because children should be doing this throughout their practical working.

Each introductory section also references the units of work described in Chapter 5 on art-focused and cross curricular topics.

Picture 1

French or English (13-14th C.): Silver-gilt casket (c.1300).
British Museum, London; 7.2 x 8.5 x 4.2cm; silver and gilt.

AT1 main focus

POS: **(i)** *select and record images and ideas from first-hand observation*
(ii) *respond to memory and imagination using a range of media*
(viii) *experiment with pattern and texture in designing and making images and artefacts*
(x) *plan and make three-dimensional structures using various materials and for a variety of purposes*

Art topic work/cross curricular links

The activities suggested can form part of art-focused topics on Working in Three Dimensions and Art for a Purpose; see pages 26 and 27.
The picture can also be used for work in History, focusing on artefacts; see page 28 for suggestions.

Background information

This little casket (approximately 7 x 8.5 x 4cm) is cast in silver which has then been covered with a layer of gold. The patterns have been **engraved** on it. It would have been made by a goldsmith. Goldsmiths worked in both silver and gold – there was no separate word for silversmiths at this time. Gold in particular was highly prized and regarded as suitable for church vessels and for use by kings and noblemen.

The casket, or 'chrismatory' was a container for holy oils. The word chrismatory comes from the Greek *chrisma*, meaning anointing or unction. Holy oils would have been a consecrated mixture of oil and balm, used for baptisms and confirmations, etc. (Balm comes from Balsam – an aromatic resinous gum exuded from certain trees and used in perfumery and medicine.)

This casket is around 700 years old. It is possible to date it and to say to whom it probably belonged because of the **heraldry** on the lid. This shows the Arms of England with the Arms of France.

The three lions represented the Royal Arms of England. They were first used by King Richard I (1189-99). The heraldic way of describing them is: three lions *or* (gold), *passant* (walking to *dexter** side with three paws

40

on the ground and the right fore-paw raised), *guardant* (depicted with body sideways but with the face towards the spectator). On this casket the lions are halved (**dimidiated**) with the fleur-de-lis (lilies) of France. This is putting it simply. Experts reading other signs think that this casket is likely to have been a gift from Margaret, the second wife of Edward I of England to Isabella of France on the occasion of her betrothal to the future Edward II of England.

*dexter is Latin for right, yet the lions on this casket appear to be walking to the left! The explanation is that in heraldry, dexter means on the right-hand side of a shield – i.e. to the spectator's left.

Discussion

1. Ask the children what they think this object is. Get them to work out that it is a box. Talk about its shape – it is rather like a house except it has legs. (Legs would make it easier to pick up off a flat surface.) Point out the fastener at the front and explain that the 'roof' is hinged at the back.

2. Ask the children to guess what it is made of and then explain that it is silver covered with gold. It would be heavy.

3. Encourage the children to describe the decoration. They may recognise the lower pattern as similar to church windows. Point out the **symmetry**. Introduce words such as 'symmetrical' and 'gothic' if appropriate. Ask them to look carefully at the heraldry on the lid – to spot the lions which are halved with the French lilies.

4. Ask what sort of person might have a box like this and what type of things might be kept in it. What would the children keep in it if it were theirs? Where would they keep it in their home?

5. Discuss why so few things like this survive from the past. Talk about how precious metals get melted down and turned into other things in time of need, or when they go out of fashion.

6. Talk about heraldry and coats of arms. Discuss why arms were important in medieval times. Point out that some people still have coats of arms nowadays. Have the children seen the Royal Arms (with the Lion and Unicorn) on anything?

Practical activities

1. Copy the patterns on the box. Start with the gothic window-like ones. Copy them exactly – they are more complicated than they seem at first glance.

2. Make up a coat of arms for yourself. It should, if possible, relate to your name in some way. For example, someone whose surname is Flower might include a flower in their coat of arms. Sometimes families adopt a short motto too, such as *Deeds not Words*. Try to make up a motto to go with your coat of arms.

3. Make a box reminiscent of this one out of card, using the template on page 150. Paint it gold or cover it with gold paper and decorate it. Make sure the decorations fit and are symmetrical. If you have designed your own coat of arms you could put this on the lid.

4. Think of a building you know and make a box to look like it. Decorate the outside of the box with images of all the things that might be going on inside the building. Talk about boxes or containers where you see the inside on the outside, e.g. baked bean tins.

5. Talk about things you have that are special to you. If you have a special box to put things in, bring it to school and compare it to those of your friends. Make a box to put something special in. Embellish it with decorations such as bits of shiny material, glass beads etc.

Cross refer to the *Luttrel Psalter* (Picture 39), which was produced in about 1340. A link can be made between the writing of a motto and its illumination.

Cross refer to the heraldry mentioned in Lippi's 'Portrait of a Man and Woman' (Picture 40), gold and silver mining in the *Kuttenberg Kanzional* (Picture 5), the bronze aquamanile (Picture 10).

Picture 2

Edouard Vuillard (1868-1940): Woman in Blue with a Child (c.1899).
Glasgow Museums, Glasgow; 48.6 x 56.5cm; oil on cardboard.

AT1 main focus

POS: (i) *select and record images and ideas from first-hand observation*
(ii) *respond to memory and imagination using a range of media*
(vii) *apply the principles of colour mixing in making various kinds of images*
(viii) *experiment with pattern and texture in designing and making images and artefacts*

Art topic work/cross curricular links

The activities suggested can form part of an art-focused topic on Images of Self and the Family; see page 20.

Background information

Vuillard was one of a small group of artists called the Nabis or 'prophets' founded in 1892 by students of the Academie Julien in Paris. The name was chosen to indicate their forward outlook and the inspiration they took from Paul Gauguin's work. Like Gauguin, they were influenced by medieval enamels and stained glass, and emphasised bold shapes, strong colour and a flattening out of form in their paintings. They were keen to develop their ideas in designing different types of work such as decorative screens, posters, book illustrations and stage sets. The Nabis (who included Vuillard's friend and fellow artist Pierre Bonnard), in representing what they saw as flat coloured patterns, helped develop the idea and style of **abstract** painting.

Vuillard painted the places and people most familiar to him which give his works an attractive intimacy. His favourite subjects were his studio, the apartment in which he lived as a bachelor with his mother and other members of his family, and friends.

Discussion

1. Ask the children what catches their eye when first looking at the picture. Is it a particular colour, pattern, or shape? Is it the baby, the mother or the cats? What is the mother helping the baby to do? Are the cats taking much notice? Why not?

2. Talk about what kind of room this is. Can the children see the following pieces of furniture:

    A bed/chaise-longue with cushions?
    A folding screen?
    A tall plant pot stand with splayed legs?
    A framed picture on the wall?

How can you tell this is in one corner of the room? Is there a sense of space in the room – enough to make you feel you could walk around in it? How many different patterns can you see? Have you ever seen a room like this? Does it look comfortable and cosy? How would you describe it? Would you like a room like this?

3. Do the children think the artist painted exactly what he saw or do they think he changed some of the colours and patterns for this picture?

4. Discuss the chunky style of painting in which you can see very clearly how the artist has built up the work. Note that the artist has used a mid-toned **ground** (basic overall colour), so that much of the effect of the painting relies on the use of **opaque** colour standing out against the ground. Talk about the way the work is divided up into a series of **planes** or areas of **tone** and how the patterning is then applied within each area. The pattern of the material on the bed, for instance, is sunlit at the top and at the bottom, but in shadow in the middle, so that it gets a different set of colours here. The light warm tones become much deeper in the centre of the bed. Look carefully with the children at how the patterns have been painted. On the wall above the baby's head, the yellow has been painted first and then the pattern has been applied over the top. However, on the bed the pale tone is painted carefully around the floral shapes.

5. Ask the children which colours seem to stand out and why. (Emphasise the use of **primary colours.**)

Practical activities

1. Make a viewfinder by cutting a small square hole in a piece of card. Look through the viewfinder at one corner of the classroom and draw the outlines of the main shapes you can see on a piece of paper. Then fill in each shape with different patterns using coloured crayons or felt-tips.

2. Follow the same process as above, but instead of colouring in the shapes, cut them out of wallpaper samples or scraps of material to make a colourful collage of the corner of the room. Choose contrasting patterns and colours.

3. Everyone in the class could bring in a piece of patterned material. These could then be cut into simple geometrical shapes and stuck down to make a large frieze like a patchwork quilt. This activity could also involve some work on the origins of different materials and motifs.

4. Experiment with different ways of painting patterns. For example, do a **still life** of flowers on a piece of material with a floral pattern.

Follow up

1. Compare the picture by Vuillard with photographs of interiors of rooms from the same period, i.e. late 19th century and/or up to the present day, which include lots of pattern.

2. For other images focusing on pattern see William Morris's, tapestry (Picture 28), Boccaccio's *De Claris Mulieribus* (Picture 19), and Delacroix's sketch of a Moorish interior (Picture 30).

Picture 3

Pieter Bruegel (1525-1569): The Fall of Icarus (c.1558).
Musées Royaux des Beaux Arts de Belgiques, Brussels; 73.5 x 112cm; oil on canvas.

AT1 main focus

POS: **(ii)**   *respond to memory and imagination using a range of media*
       (ix)   *experiment with ways of representing shape, form and space*
       (x)   *plan and make three-dimensional structures using various materials and for a
variety of purposes*

Art topic work/cross curricular links

The activities suggested can form part of an art-focused topic on Aspects of Landscape;
see page 22.
The picture can also be used as a stimulus for creative writing; see page 32.

Background information

Pieter Bruegel the Elder was the first, and by far the most important of
a Flemish family of painters. He is also sometimes known as 'Peasant
Bruegel'. He had two painter sons Pieter and Jan who normally spell
their surname with an 'h' – Brueghel. This does not entirely clarify
things however, as the father also used the 'h' until 1559! Bruegel the
Elder is well known for painting **landscapes**, peasant village scenes,
religious subjects and allegories.

The original story of the Fall of Icarus is found in Ovid *Metamorphoses
VIII: 183-235*. (It is available in the *Penguin Classics* series).

Daedelus was a legendary Athenian craftsman who created the
labyrinthine palace on the Island of Crete, in which King Minos kept
the Minotaur. He is also credited with inventing various tools such as
the saw, axe and gimlet. Daedelus and his son Icarus were imprisoned
by Minos on Crete but escaped using wings which Daedelus constructed.
These wings were made of feathers, some of which were attached with
thread, others with wax. (Ovid gives a graphic description which is
worth looking up.) Despite Daedelus's warning: 'Icarus, you must
follow a course midway between earth and heaven in case the sun
should scorch your feathers if you go too high, or the water make them

heavy if you are too low', Icarus flew too near the sun. The wax on his wings melted and he fell into the sea and drowned.

Moralists have used the story in various ways; for example to demonstrate the dangers of going to extremes, and the follies of the young who do not listen to those who are older and more experienced. Bruegel may have used the myth to illustrate a Flemish proverb, 'Not a plough stands still when a man dies'. There is a dead body just visible above the horse's head.

Discussion

1. Discuss how everything in this **composition** leads towards the sun. The ploughman leads the horse down and round, with the furrows pointing towards the sheep and the large boat, whose sails have caught the wind so that it is being driven out to sea towards the sun. Similarly the land in the distance both right and left curves in towards the fierce bright light which has melted Icarus's wings.

2. The drama occurs within a scene in which everything carries on as normal. Indeed, the wide sweep of the composition seems to encompass the whole range of everyday life: the countryside is cultivated, the sheep are grazing, the ships are trading between the various ports and in the towns we imagine life carrying on in the normal way. The shepherd is looking up but not at Icarus. His attention may be caught by a bird or a movement on a distant hill. The splashdown in the bottom right corner is all the more poignant for being largely unobserved. A solitary sheep looks towards the figure in the sea, and a figure on the rocks above appears to reach out ineffectually. The boat which might have helped, has the wind in its sails and is sailing out to sea away from the hapless Icarus. The dreams and aspirations of Icarus, and of humankind, are set against a practical and living world in which the daily round of everyday life presents an altogether separate reality.

Practical activities

1. The tale of Daedelus and his son's escape from Crete could be told before the children see this picture. They could even be invited to illustrate the story themselves from their imagination. In these circumstances Bruegel's treatment of the subject will probably both surprise and amuse them.

2. See if the children can work out a moral to the story for themselves. Ask them to make up a contemporary story that has the same message and to illustrate it. (A strip cartoon might be most effective here.)

3. Talk about events in life that effect some people deeply and others not at all. It may be a death in one family in the community, or a tragedy affecting millions of people in a remote country. Try to make a piece of work that explores this idea. It may take the form of a poster designed to make people aware of the implications of events going on somewhere else in the world.

4. Talk about wings. Is it really possible to make wings out of feathers, thread and wax? Why not? What is special about feathers? (They are light yet very strong.) How are birds' bodies adapted to flight? Collect some feathers. Study them carefully and make detailed pencil drawings in a sketch-book showing the quill, shaft and vanes of barbs.

5. This activity is recommended for 9-11 year olds only. If working on the Minotaur myth, make a model of a labyrinth. Construct it on a large sheet of card – or on several small ones joined together. Model the palace using toy bricks, small boxes (such as match boxes), clay or Plasticene. Plan the rooms so that they have odd entrance positions and crazy passages between them. Remember that the layout should be like a maze.

Look for photographs of the excavations at Knossos (in Crete) which is almost certainly the legendary Minoan palace. Make models of the Minotaur, King Minos, Theseus, Ariadne with her ball of twine, Daedelus and Icarus. Place them inside the labyrinth.

Cross refer to other landscape pictures which tell a story: Lorraine's 'Seaport' (Picture 24), Martin's 'The Bard' (Picture 8) and the Persian miniature (Picture 9).

Cross refer to other pictures depicting characters from Greek mythology: Hora (Picture 6), Guercino's 'Aurora' (Picture 33).

Picture 4

Thomas Gainsborough (1727-88): Mr and Mrs Andrews (c.1750).
National Gallery, London: 69.8 x 119.4cm; oil on canvas.

AT1 main focus

POS: **(i)** *select and record images from first-hand observation*
(iii) *use a sketch-book to record observations and ideas*
(vi) *experiment with different qualities of line and tone in making images*
(vii) *apply the principles of colour mixing in making various kinds of images*

Art topic work/cross curricular links

The images suggested can form part of an art-focused topic on Observing and Responding; see page 23.
The picture can also be linked with Geography fieldwork; see page 33.

Background information

Thomas Gainsborough was one of the leading British painters of the 18th century. He developed an interest in drawing at an early age and filled many sketch-books with drawings of natural forms and views of the countryside around his native village of Sudbury in Suffolk. He then trained as a painter in London and his interest in **landscapes** was fuelled by the example of 17th-century Dutch paintings which he saw in the auction houses there. He returned to Suffolk where he soon established a reputation for painting excellent 'likenesses' (i.e. **portraits**) which guaranteed his success when he moved to the fashionable city of Bath. He reluctantly acknowledged the fact that to make a living as a painter in Britain he had to paint what people wanted most and that was portraits. By providing an outdoor setting for many of his portraits, however, he combined his own interests with those of his patrons.

It is tempting to suggest that Gainsborough deliberately placed Mr and Mrs Robert Andrews at the left in this picture so that he could indulge his own interest in landscape on the right, but he would not have been able to do this so blatantly without their consent. In fact the landscape, recognisable as Aubries, their farm near Sudbury, was an important asset and status symbol for the Andrews. The neat furrows of the field and carefully stacked sheaves along with the enclosed fields where sheep and cattle graze, demonstrate up-to-date farming practices in tune with contemporary agricultural reforms. Progressive agricultural reform was actively encouraged by the reigning king, George III, who earned the nickname 'Farmer George'.

The landscape setting also provided the opportunity to include another status symbol, since contemporary game laws precluded anyone below a certain social standing from shooting game. It seems more natural to find Robert Andrews posing outside with his gun, his dog and the bag of shot suspended from his belt, than if he was shown inside. The game may be on Mrs Andrews's lap but this area of the painting is unfinished.

The couple are fashionably dressed. Gainsborough took delight in painting fabrics and the details of folds (unlike some of his contemporaries who employed drapery painters to paint these bits for them). His paintings therefore provide fascinating insight into contemporary costume. Mrs Andrews's dress would have been shaped with whalebone or reed paniers (baskets) on either side, attached to a hoop worn rather like an underskirt. At the height of this particular fashion, women's dresses could be up to five metres wide!

The bench may be Gainsborough's own invention rather than based on an actual design since it is rather more elaborate than most contemporary wooden benches, and wrought iron work did not come into fashion for another 20 years.

Gainsborough would not have painted the Andrews outside. They would have posed for their portraits in his studio. He would most probably have painted the landscape in the studio too from a sketch/sketches made outside.

Discussion

1.   Ask the children why they think the artist painted this picture with the canvas this way round, i.e. **horizontally** rather than **vertically**? (The emphasis for most **full-length portraits** at the time was vertical.)

2.   Encourage the children to look closely at the people in the picture. Do they look relaxed and happy? Does one look more relaxed than the other? If so, which one and why? Can you tell what these people might have been like from their expressions, their clothes, or the way they are sitting/standing?

What do you think was going to be on Mrs Andrews's lap? Could it be something Mr Andrews had given to her? Why do you think this bit is unfinished? What would you put there?

Do you think it would be easy for Mrs Andrews to walk around and go through doorways in this dress? She is sitting on a bench outside but what sort of furniture could she sit on inside? What sort of material does the dress look as if it is made from?

3.   How would the children describe the colour of the dress? Point out that it is used to complement the colour of the cornfield. Is it a **warm** or a **cool colour**? Another artist, Sir Joshua Reynolds, working at the same time as Gainsborough, recommended that painters use warm colours in the **foreground** and cool colours in the **background** to emphasise the sense of space in their paintings and make people stand out.

Do the children think the painting would have looked worse/just as good/better if Gainsborough had painted Mrs Andrews in a pink dress? Has the artist introduced any warm colours in the foreground? Where? (Look at the poppies, shoes, earth, crops etc.) What helps lead your eyes into the distance? What draws attention to the church tower?

4.   What time of year do the children think this is and what is the weather like? Why do they think the Andrews are shown beneath a tree?

5.   How many of the things in this painting do the children think are based on direct observation and how many, if any, on imagination?

Practical activities

1.   Paint your own version of Mr and Mrs Andrews but try a vertical portrait. What would you have to leave out, and what would there be more of?

2.   Paint an updated view of this couple. What would they look like now and what sort of things would they have with them? What kind of environment do you think they would be in? Do you think they would have the same sort of dog or perhaps a different pet?

3.   Design some more furniture for Mrs Andrews, bearing in mind the width of her dress.

4.   Two people in the class could pose like Mr and Mrs Andrews while the others draw them. How easy is it to keep these positions? Imagine the conversation that they might have between themselves and with the artist.

5.   Look at the unpainted area in Mrs Andrews's lap. Notice how it is a darker **tone** than the white which is used to paint her bodice, or the **highlights** on her dress, or even her flesh tones. This is the overall underlying colour with which Gainsborough has painted his canvas before beginning the painting. Try working a painting up from a similar background colour.

6.   Try painting from direct observation. Use a piece of tree bark, a few stalks of corn or stems of long grasses, or a piece of silky material.

7.   Make some sketches of a view outside using either a pencil or a paint brush and paints. Pay particular attention to the sky and any trees you can see. In a sketch remember that you do not need to include everything in great detail.

Cross refer to Constable's 'Cloud Studies' (Pictures 16 and 17).

Picture 5

Matthew of Kuttenberg (15th C.): Frontispiece of the *Kuttenberg Kanzional* (Ms Cod. 15.501, fol.1v.), (c.1490). Osterreichische Nationalbibliothek, Vienna; 69 x 45cm (whole page); illuminated manuscript (tempera and gold leaf on parchment).

AT1 main focus

POS: **(i)**   *select and record images and ideas from first-hand observation*

        (ii)   *respond to memory and imagination using a range of media*

        (iv)   *experiment with ideas suggested by different source materials and explain how they have used them to develop their work*

        (ix)   *experiment with ways of representing shape, form and space*

Art topic work/cross curricular links

The activities suggested can form part of an art-focused topic on Telling a Story; see page 21.

Background information

This is the frontispiece of a book by one Matthew of Kuttenberg. It shows a silver mine at Kuttenberg in Bavaria about 50 miles east of Prague. The mine was at one time the richest in Europe. This remarkable frontispiece shows the full story of ore extraction from the underground mine, the crushing of the ore, and the grading and selling of it. The elaborate scene has been given a frame surmounted by a shield, held by angels, which displays a **gilded** 'W'. This W probably relates to the name of the person who commissioned the work.

Very little gold was mined in central and western Europe during the medieval period – most gold was from recycled treasures from the ancient world. However, in the 14th and 15th centuries there was a need for more precious metals, and mining in Europe increased. About a quarter of the silver produced at this mine is thought to have been minted, the rest was exported in bars.

Discussion

1.   This picture is rather like those **cross-section** books with which the children may be familiar. Discuss the arrangement of the picture: it shows an interior view, an exterior view and an underground view all at the same time. The underground part is a cross-section and the central portion is an **aerial view**. Talk about the idea of cross-sections, beginning with simple objects such as fruit and vegetables. Explain what an aerial view is, perhaps using the term 'bird's-eye view'. Point out the advantage of using an aerial view to show more clearly what is going on.

2.   Get the children to describe what each of the miners is doing. Let a different child describe each. How are the miners dressed? Are they dressed differently from the other people in the picture and if so, why?

3.   Ask the children to work out what all the other people are up to.

4.   Can they see any animals?

5.   Play counting games: how many baskets? etc.

6.   Who do they think has the funniest hat? the nastiest job? the nicest job? the fewest clothes on? Who is making the most noise? etc.

7.   Which of these people would they most/least like to be – and why?

8.   Broaden out the discussion. What is under the ground where the children are now? If in a first floor classroom (or higher) there are probably other people underneath. If on the ground floor what is below? (Gas/electric ducts, water pipes, drainage and sewers.) Is the building the first on the site? If not, there might be foundations of older ones and things that people have left behind. Is there any metal to be mined under the school? If not, what is between the school building and the earth's core?

Practical activities

This is a picture which lends itself to both group work and to considerations of scale. Being a manuscript **illumination** the original is, of course, relatively small.

1.   Give the children a piece of A4 paper – ideally with a ready drawn frame. (There is a template on page 151.) Ask them to draw a scene with lots of busy little people in it, each doing something different. If seen slightly from above the children will not have problems of overlapping. An obvious choice of subject would be children in a playground. (Other paintings you could look at for use here, although not included in this book, are various scenes by Lowry and Bruegel. The picture by Avercamp in the *Approaches to Art, Key Stage One* would also be helpful.)

2.   Make studies of simple cross-sections, such as fruit and vegetables. Then go on to look at more complicated cross-sections, boats, cars etc. Go to local museums and look at the kinds of cross-sections they display there, including **dioramas** which show things underground like rabbit burrows or layers of different kinds of rocks.

3.   Make up some imaginary cross-sections. Imagine, for example, that inside a large stone is a secret world of some kind. Make drawings or paintings showing what you think might be there.

4. This scene shows many of the aspects of a single industry. Is there an industry associated with your local area which you could explore to research all the stages of manufacture and put together as a diorama, with models, painted figures and backgrounds?

5. For group work, make an attempt at a cross-section of the school. (This is quite difficult and therefore we recommend this activity for children aged 9 to 11 years.)

i)   Choose the viewpoint. If possible, go outside and draw the school from the view you are going to use. Ideally this should include the children's own classroom. Each child should draw the view.

ii)   Back in the classroom, discuss what you would see if you took away the walls. The discussion is essential to thinking about structure and how buildings are put together, what is in the wall cavities and so on. If you are lucky you might have a demolition site nearby so that you can see these things.

iii)   Invite the children to draw their view of the school again – with the wall missing – and to put the people in.

The effect will be rather like looking into an open doll's house and children may find it helpful to think in those terms. But make sure they think about what a doll's house does not have in terms of beams and rafters, drains and service ducts. Dolls' houses only display what we normally *see*.

Cross refer to the silver-gilt casket (Picture 1) as an example of a silver object from the same period as the *Kuttenberg Kanzional*.

Picture 6

Greek (c.1st century B.C.): Dancing Hora from the Theatre of Dionysos, Athens.
National Archaeological Museum, Athens; 112 x 63cm; stone.

AT1 main focus

POS: **(i)** *select and record images and ideas from first-hand observation*

(v) *apply their knowledge and experience of different materials, tools and techniques using them experimentally and expressively*

(viii) *experiment with pattern and texture in designing and making images and artefacts*

Art topic work/cross curricular links

The activities suggested can form part of an art-focused topic on Work in Three Dimensions; see page 26.

Background information

The Greek word from which the Horae derive their name, signifies a period of time. This can be applied to years, the seasons or the hours of the day. Because of these different meanings, there have been various ways of representing the Horae. Generally speaking, in mythology, they were sister spirits who usually personified the seasons and who gave their name to the hours. Confusingly their number varies between two and eleven or twelve – different writers give different numbers.

The Horae were the female attendants of Eos (Roman: Aurora) goddess of the dawn, and of Selene (Roman: Luna) goddess of the Moon. They also formed part of the retinue of Aphrodite (Roman: Venus) along with the Three Graces. They watched over people's morals and 'mellowed the behaviour of men'. They were also protectors of youth. Another of their duties was to guard the gates of heaven which they opened (or closed) to the Immortals by removing or replacing a thick cloud!

The Horae are normally depicted as young women, holding in their hands the products of various seasons, such as flowers, branches or ears of corn. This Hora wears a flimsy *himation* (the outer garment of the Ancient Greeks) which waves in the wind as she dances – they were reputed to dance a lot. The carving dates from the 1st century B.C. and was discovered in 1862. There is a small amount of damage on her face and part of the lower portion of her body is missing.

This is an example of **relief** carving in which the design, or in this case figure, stands out from a flat surface. **Low relief** is shallow and **high relief** is more three dimensional.

Discussion

The Horae are not very central in Greek mythology and there is confusion about their number and their names. If you are going to use this image in connection with the ancient Greeks we suggest you talk about the Horae representing the seasons and periods of time (bringing in the name-link with the hours of course).

1.   Talk about how the image was made, about high and low relief. Explain that it was hand-carved out of stone. It was part of the decoration of a theatre dedicated to Dionysus (Roman: Bacchus) in Athens, and it is about 2000 years old.

2.   Greek sculptures were often coloured (the correct term is **polychromed**). Ask the children which colours would suit this figure. If this figure was once coloured, what do they think has happened to the colours? Discuss whether the Hora looks happy, sad or pensive etc. What sort of dance do the children think she is doing?

3.   Look at the extraordinary flowing movement and rhythm of the drapery and ask the children what it reminds them of. They may say waves, clothes on a washing line in the wind, or just the notion of the wind itself. Discuss the fact that this is carved in stone and about the way this hard and heavy material appears to have been transformed into something much lighter and more ethereal, and yet cannot be mistaken for anything other than stone. Think of the way other hard and heavy materials are made to seem light. Ask the children to suggest some objects – such as boats and aeroplanes – which float and fly, yet are made of steel. Much art is based around the notion that the artist transforms a basic material into something new or at least suggests it. Talk about the particular characteristics of this drapery which suggest lightness and lift, the way the curves have been created to suggest air beneath them like parachutes. (For comparison, look at Picture 26 'A Wild Sea at Chōshi', and Botticelli's 'Primavera' in *Approaches to Art, Key Stage One*.)

4.   Following on from the idea that the wind itself is represented by its effect on this drapery, talk about the way we might represent abstract notions like happiness or fear which are only visible in their effects but not in themselves.

Practical activities

1.   Photocopy the Hora and let each child have a copy. Cut her out and glue her into the middle of a page. Then give her an environment. Where will she be? How will you represent the wind blowing her garments out behind her?

2. In small groups or pairs, make reliefs of figures using Plasticene, clay or another modelling material – you could use dough and bake and eat the results! Make them on a flat board such as stiff cardboard. Choose subjects that (unlike this Hora) are designed to be seen from above.

Start with a thick flat lump of modelling material, and shape it with your fingers to get the main forms. Use tools (improvise here) for the finer details. It is important that the children understand that they are not making a drawing with lines, but are modelling. Talk about this, and demonstrate (after some practise!) what you have in mind.

3. As a group, make a relief which suggests movement of figures in water, rather than wind, for contrast. Encourage the children to observe the effects of water on fabrics when they are soaked, before starting the model. (Wearing floppy T-shirts in a swimming pool will give an obvious effect.)

Cross refer to Guercino's 'Aurora' (Picture 33) as another depiction of characters from Greek mythology.

Cross refer to the Assyrian relief sculpture (Picture 19) in *Approaches to Art, Key Stage One*.

Picture 7

Henry Moore (1898-86): King and Queen (1952-3).
Glenkiln Farm Estate, Dumfries, Scotland; height 164cm; bronze.

AT1 main focus

POS: **(iv)** *experiment with ideas suggested by different source materials and explain how they have used them to develop their work*

(v) *apply their knowledge and experience in different materials, tools and techniques, using them experimentally and expressively*

(viii) *experiment with pattern and texture in designing and making various kinds of images*

(ix) *experiment with ways of representing shape, form and space*

(x) *plan and make three-dimensional structures using various materials and for a variety of purposes*

Art topic work/cross curricular links

The activities suggested can form part of art-focused topics on Work in Three Dimensions and Aspects of Landscape; see pages 26 and 22.

Background information

Henry Moore was one of the outstanding British sculptors of this century. He combined a love of traditional materials and methods of working in wood, stone and bronze with new ideas rooted in **abstract** art. His favourite subject, however, was the human figure and even in his most abstract pieces there is often some reference to the human figure which is readily identifiable.

The artist believed firmly in a close kinship between human forms and natural forms in the landscape, and considered a natural setting to be ideal for his sculpture. He was delighted with the siting of the 'King and Queen' along with other examples of his sculpture on the Glenkiln Farm Estate. The sky, in his opinion, provided the best possible background for sculpture: 'There is no background to sculpture better than the sky, because you are contrasting solid form with its opposite, space.

57

The sculpture then has no competition, no distraction from other solid objects. If I wanted the most fool-proof background for a sculpture I would always choose the sky.' It is not surprising to find that Henry Moore preferred sculpture **in the round** (free-standing) to **relief** sculpture. He did not wish his sculpture to be constrained or confined by the wall of, or alcove set into, a building.

Henry Moore was born in Castleford, Yorkshire and turned to sculpture as a student at the Leeds School of Art. He went on to the Royal College of Art in London and later became a member of staff there. The single most important influence on his own work was the sculpture of Michelangelo, but he was also inspired by examples of Ancient Egyptian, Ancient Greek, African and Mexican sculpture, which he saw both in Britain and on visits abroad. Furthermore, he developed many ideas for sculpture through drawing from natural forms such as weathered stones, shells and bones, gnarled tree trunks and pieces of driftwood, exploring them from a variety of angles to get a full sense of their existence in the round.

Moore was 54 when he produced the 'King and Queen' and a well established figure in artistic circles. He had already enjoyed a retrospective exhibition of his work at the South Bank, London, which also helped mark the Festival of Britain in 1951. In the 1950s he used bronze in preference to other media for sculpture. He would first model his ideas in clay – often on a much smaller scale than the final version – and then enlarge the model to full size and cast it in bronze with the help of a team of assistants. (A clear explanation of the process of bronze casting is given in the *Oxford Dictionary of Art*.)

Five editions of the 'King and Queen' were made. The green colouring visible on the sculpture is called the **patina**. When bronze is exposed to the air for a long time this patina develops naturally, but because of the time involved it was sometimes induced artificially by sculptors. In this case the patina complements the **landscape** setting and adds an air of timelessness to the figures: they could almost be 'as old as the hills'. The title 'King and Queen' was given by Henry Moore to provide a way into looking at and exploring the sculpture.

Discussion

1. Talk about what makes these figures look like human beings. The artist called them 'King and Queen'. Ask the children what makes them look regal: their appearance/the way they are sitting/what they are sitting on/where they are sitting.

Moore decided to give the king a crown and a beard. What shapes suggest these features? Do the children think the queen looks more realistic than the king or not? Why? What has the artist done to suggest their clothes? What has he done to suggest their eyes?

2. Henry Moore could be asking why a king and queen should look different from any other couple. Here, there is a sense that we could be looking at any couple quietly contemplating the view. Like anyone else, they each have their own characteristic posture, with the woman dignified, alert and straight-backed and the man a tall, thin, slightly curving figure with long limbs and big hands. Discuss which aspects of the figures seem the most unusual. The answer will probably be the heads. Talk about what the heads remind one of. It might, in the case of the king, be a frog or an alien, or a helmet of some kind. It might even be a bone.

3.   Moore was interested in exploring the idea of opposites in this piece of sculpture. Discuss how many opposites seem to be included here: male/female; solid form/open space; smooth texture/rough texture; realistic detail/abstract shape.

4.   Imagine what it would be like to walk around this sculpture and see it from different viewpoints. Why do the children think the photograph of it was taken from this viewpoint? What do the king and queen appear to be looking at?

5.   The artist really liked the fact that his sculpture could be seen in the open air. What makes the king and queen seem to fit in with their surroundings? (Encourage the children to think about the shapes and colours of the sculpture and the landscape.)

Practical activities

1.   Make your own small-scale version of a king and queen out of clay. Will you add more or less detail to your figures? How will you suggest their faces or facial features? Will you make some bits look more realistic than others? What will you sit them on?

If you want to give your king and queen a long cloak or robe try rolling out slabs of clay thinly (like pastry) then pressing hessian or some other textured material into the clay, to leave an imprint of texture. Then wrap the thin sheet of clay around the figure arranging the folds carefully.

2.   Imagine the conversation the king and queen might be having: Are they admiring the view? Do you think they look comfortable? Then paint a picture for or about them – perhaps a different view for them to look at, or a more comfortable throne etc.

3.   Make a collection of pictures and models of kings and queens, including playing cards, chess pieces and other images rather than portraits of specific kings and queens. Compare the differences and similarities in their appearances. Would they be instantly recognisable as kings and queens? Why? (This activity particularly addresses the requirements of AT2 POS i, 'compare the different purposes of familiar visual forms and discuss their findings with their teachers and peers'.)

4.   After discussing the heads of the king and queen, find and draw objects that suggest heads or faces to you, for example bits of bone or stones. One contemporary artist has used bread dough to make heads. He then bakes the bread and has the result cast in metal. You could try the first stages of this.

5.   Make some careful drawings from natural forms such as shells, stones or driftwood, observing the play of light and shadow on and around the objects. Make drawings of the same form from a variety of viewpoints on the same sheet of paper to show it 'in the round'.

6.   Make a model of one of the natural forms you have drawn out of clay or Plasticene. Does the shape remind you of anything else or suggest another sort of form? Can you turn it into a human form?

Cross refer to other figures in landscapes: Gainsborough's 'Mr and Mrs Andrews' (Picture 4), Martin's 'The Bard' (Picture 8), 'Baz Bahadur and Rupmati' (Picture 9).

59

Picture 8

John Martin (1789-1854): The Bard (1817).
Laing Art Gallery, Newcastle-upon-Tyne; 213.5 x 155cm: oil on canvas.

AT1 main focus

POS: **(ii)** *respond to memory and imagination using a range of media*
(ix) *experiment with ways of representing shape, form and space*

Art topic work/cross curricular links

The activities suggested can form part of art-focused topics on Telling a Story and Imagination and Invention; see pages 21 and 24.

Background information

This picture illustrates a poem called *The Bard* by Thomas Gray which was published in 1757. The painting was exhibited at the Royal Academy in 1817. John Martin, the artist, (nicknamed 'Mad Martin') was born into a very poor family living in Northumberland. He is particularly well known for his enormous, spectacular, melodramatic landscapes, usually crowded with tiny figures and illustrating some historical or biblical narrative.

Bards were the ancient Celtic minstrels and poets. They celebrated the victories of heroes, incited their people to battle, acted as heralds and performed at banquets etc.

The poem and the painting tell the (untrue) story of how Edward I of England (reigned 1272-1307), during his campaign against the Welsh, reputedly condemned all the bards to death. This was to prevent the bards from nurturing the spirit of resistance among the Welsh people.

In Martin's picture, the last bard, high on a rock above the river Conway, curses Edward and the English troops before throwing himself into the foaming river below. The picture was exhibited with a quotation from the poem which gives the words the bard is supposed to be uttering.

The first two lines are:

> 'Ruin seize thee, ruthless King.
> Confusion on thy banners wait;'

Martin has followed the description in the poem quite closely. Here is another section of it:

> '. . . on a rock, whose haughty brow
> Frowns o're old Conway's foaming flood,
> Robed in the sable garb of woe,
> With haggard eyes the Poet stood;
> (Loose his beard, and hoary hair,
> Streamed, like a meteor, to the troubled air;)
> And with a master's hand, and prophet's fire,
> Struck the deep sorrows of his lyre.'

Discussion

1.   Ask the children what they can see. Let them take turns to spot something in the picture which has not previously been mentioned, so that they become familiar with the image.

Ask what this kind of image reminds the children of e.g. imagery from films, cartoons or computer game backgrounds etc.

2.   Explain the historical background to this picture. Edward I, King of England, was determined to extend his power into Wales, so he waged a series of campaigns against the Welsh. The most famous of which was against Llewelyn, Prince of Gwynedd, of north-west Wales. Llewelyn was driven back to Snowdonia and eventually forced to surrender to the English. In order to maintain his authority in Wales, Edward built a series of huge castles, these included Conway, Caernarfon, Harlech and Beaumaris. Today most of these castles are in ruins, but Martin's picture shows a castle (based on Harlech castle) as it might have been in the Middle Ages.

Ask the children where they would site a castle to give it the greatest advantage over an enemy force.

3.   Talk about the scenery in Wales. If possible, find some postcards of the mountainous regions and ask the children to compare the actual Welsh landscape to that depicted by Martin. (Martin's mountains look more like the Alps than the Cambrian mountains or Snowdonia!) Discuss the artist's reasons for romanticising the landscape.

4.   Explain to the children what a bard is. Can they identify him? How is he dressed? What is he carrying? What might he be saying? Recite the words that the poet gave him to say.

Talk about the poetical description of the bard. Make sure the children understand the terms used, such as 'haughty brow', and explain that the Conway is a river. The word 'sable' means black. (It is also the **heraldic** word for black. Some cross reference can be made to the heraldic terms mentioned on pages 40 and 41). 'Garb' of course means clothes, and 'hoary' (of hair) means grey or white with age.

Compare the poem with the picture. Ask the children whether the details match exactly. (The main difference is that the artist has given the bard a harp and not a lyre which is smaller.)

61

5. Talk about the **composition** of the picture. How has the artist achieved a sense of the towering cliffs and mountains with the precipitous rock faces? Compare the composition with that of Picture 3 'The Fall of Icarus', which (is very different but) leads to a similarly bright sun in the distant peaks. Follow the path as high as you can go. Are the figures on horses going up or coming down? Notice how all the movement is down (people and water) which makes the distant peaks seem even less accessible.

6. Talk about the textures that can be seen, the craggy rock, the spongy trees with branches like blood vessels, the silky water and the foam. Discuss how all the elements are treated, earth, air, fire (sun) and water.

Practical activities

1. Make up your own story about what is going on and illustrate another scene from it.

2. For 9-11 year olds: make a similar scene as a model for a stage set or **diorama**, with flat cut-out scenery painted to look like rocks and mountains etc. and set up in receding planes with a backcloth for the sky.

3. What can the bard see? Draw the scene from his point of view looking down over the valley and river onto the troops below. Then draw Edward's viewpoint.

Picture 9

Indian (17-18th C.): Baz Bahadur, the King of Malwa in Central India 1554-61, Riding at Night with his Lover Rupmati (c.1720).
Ashmolean Museum, Oxford; 21 x 25.7cm: gouache on paper.

AT1 main focus

POS:
- (ii) *respond to memory and imagination using a range of media*
- (iv) *experiment with ideas suggested by different source materials and explain how they have used them to develop their work*
- (v) *apply their knowledge and experience of different materials, tools and techniques, using them experimentally and expressively*
- (viii) *experiment with pattern and texture in designing and making images and artefacts*
- (ix) *experiment with ways of representing shape, form and space*

Art topic work/cross curricular links

The activities suggested can form part of an art-focused topic on Telling a Story; see page 21.
The picture can also be used as a stimulus for imaginative writing; see page 32.

Background information

Baz Bahadur was the Muslim King of Malwa in Central India. He loved music, poetry and his favourite companion – the beautiful Hindu dancing girl, Rupmati. Baz Bahadur was overthrown in 1561 by the Mughal, General Adham Khan. Rupmati poisoned herself rather than be taken by the general and Baz Bahadur fled the kingdom. Nine years later he was admitted to the court of the Mughal Emperor Akbar and became famous for his singing. The romantic and sad story of Baz Bahadur and Rupmati became a popular theme in Indian songs and poems and was a favourite subject for court artists.

This miniature was painted by an artist attached to the Rajput Court of Kulu in the Punjab Hills when Kulu culture was at its height. The Rajputs (ruling dynasties) maintained their independence from the Mughal Court and each Rajput Court and province developed a distinctive identity from its neighbours. The high mountainous region of Kulu was described by British travellers in the 19th century, who noted its grey swirling mists and terraced orchards which were full of blossom in the spring. Trees grown included walnut, apricot, peach, quince, pine and oak, in addition to wild pomegranates, wild pears and wild figs. These seem to

63

have inspired the lovely plant designs which artists included in their narrative scenes.

Few names of court artists were recorded although thousands of paintings were produced by them. An artist would usually remain at the same court for most of his life and paint pictures to order. The most common subjects required were religious themes, pictures celebrating the local ruler and romantic themes such as this one. The training of artists tended to be a family business with styles and ways of depicting figures handed down from generation to generation. Here the figures of Baz Bahadur and Rupmati conform to tradition: they are shown riding side by side, their heads in **profile** as they gaze into each other's large eyes. His skin is darker than hers but he rides a lighter-coloured horse. Their wealth is indicated by their sumptuous clothes and the decoration of the horses' bridles and saddles.

The miniature is painted on a sheet of stiff handmade paper. The paint used was **gouache**, that is, **opaque** watercolour, sometimes called **body colour**. Gouache consists of **pigments** often mixed with white and bound together with gum arabic. The colour is therefore less **translucent** than true watercolour. However, the paint can be applied more thickly and alterations can be made more easily. Changes (i.e. **pentimenti**, see Picture 13, 'The Arnolfini Marriage') to Rupmati's horse and Baz Bahadur's profile can be seen.

Miniatures from the Punjab Hills were eagerly sought as delightful 'souvenirs' by increasing numbers of visitors to India from the 19th century on. Unfortunately, in the commercial process of dealing, much valuable information about the early history of such pictures was lost.

Discussion

1. This is a very clear precise work and it is possible for children to explore all aspects of the detail included. Ask the children to have a good look at the two people on horseback. How can they tell that they are rich? (Note their clothes, jewellery and horses.) What sort of materials could their clothes be made of? What kind of sound(s) would they make riding along? (Look at the horses' legs and bridles.)

2. How can the children tell that the king and his girlfriend really like each other? How would they describe the mood of this scene? The fact that the couple are looking at each other and thus engaged in a conversation, lifts the work from a formal depiction (if both had been looking directly ahead), to something more real and human.

3. Point out that the king is holding the horse's reigns in one hand, but ask the children why he is wearing a glove on the other hand. Can they find three birds flying in front of the horses? Why are they flying so low? (Could it be to avoid the hawk?) How can you tell that the couple are near a stream? How has the artist suggested that the countryside Baz Bahadur and Rupmati are riding in is hilly? Look at the trees and plants. Are they based on real trees and plants or purely imaginary ones? Why?

4. Talk about how many colours the artist has used for the trees and plants. Did he use a thick, heavy brush or a thin, fine one? How can you tell? Where else is there fine shading? Have a good look in particular at the heads and necks of Baz Bahadur and Rupmati and the manes of their horses.

The white paint used for the pearls has been put on thickly so that they stand out from the paper i.e. in **relief**. Why would this make them look even more sparkly? (They would catch the light.)

The region where this scene was painted was often misty. Has the artist suggested mist in the painting?

5.   Consider the implications of wealth and grandeur that the painting contains and the link between the sumptuousness of all the cultural artefacts and the abundance of nature itself. These are seen to run parallel in this work so that an idealised world is presented.

Practical activities

1.   Paint a picture of yourself and a friend outside in an imaginary secret place where there are lots of trees and plants. Imagine what you would like to do there – perhaps have a picnic or just sit and chat – and include this in your picture.

2.   Choose either Baz Bahadur or Rupmati and draw and colour a picture of them doing something else they liked. Baz Bahadur enjoyed reading, writing poetry and singing. Rupmati enjoyed dancing. Decide whether you are going to show them in **profile** or **full face** and remember to include as much detail of their clothes as possible. Try and suggest the different textures of materials and jewels.

3.   Write your own story based on what you can see in the picture and then paint a picture of another episode of your story.

4.   Imagine the conversation between Baz Bahadur and Rupmati as they are riding along and/or a conversation between the two horses. What happens next?

5.   Make a collection of leaves with as many different shapes as possible, then use them as a starting point to design some fantastic trees of your own. Experiment with different colours and, if possible, different sized brushes to make the patterns and textures of the leaves and trunks. Small groups could each work on a tree which could then be displayed in a frieze along a wall to produce a class forest.

Cross refer to other pictures of paired figures: Lippi's 'Portrait of a Woman and a Man' (Picture 40), Gainsborough's 'Mr and Mrs Andrews' (Picture 4), Moore's 'King and Queen' (Picture 7), van Eyck's 'Arnolfini Marriage' (Picture 13).

Cross refer to other narrative and landscape pictures: Martin's 'The Bard' (Picture 8), Bruegel's 'The Fall of Icarus' (Picture 3), Friedrich's 'Two Men Contemplating the Moon' (Picture 23), Sassetta's 'St Francis' (Picture 38).

Cross refer to other pictures with patterns based on natural forms: Morris's tapestry (Picture 28), *Luttrell Psalter* (Picture 39), Blake's 'The Tyger' (Picture 22), bronze aquamanile (Picture 10).

Picture 10

Germanic (15th C.): Bronze aquamanile (water jug) in the form of a horse and rider.
British Museum, London; height 31cm; bronze.

AT1 main focus

POS:
(i) *select and record images and ideas from first-hand observation*
(ii) *respond to memory and imagination using a range of media*
(iv) *experiment with ideas suggested by different source materials and explain how they have used them to develop their work*
(ix) *experiment with ways of representing shape, form and space*
(x) *plan and make three-dimensional structures using various materials and for a variety of purposes*

Art topic work/cross curricular links

The activities suggested can form part of art-focused topics on Work in Three Dimensions and Art for a Purpose; see pages 26 and 27.
The picture can also be used as part of work in History, focusing on artefacts; see page 29 for suggestions.

Background information

An aquamanile (from the latin *aqua* meaning water, and *manus* meaning hand) is a metal ewer (or water jug) which was either for use in the home, or for the liturgical ceremony of the washing of the celebrant's hands during Mass. An aquamanile often had a matching bowl. They were filled through an opening in the top (in this case through a square hole at the back of the lion's head) and emptied through a spout in the animal's mouth.

Many books about courtesy and manners from the Middle Ages stress the importance of being clean and included in this is the importance of hand washing. For example, one William Caxton advises in his *Book of Curtesye*:

> 'Washe with water your hondes so cleene
> That in the towel shal no spotte be sene.'

Hand washing took place before and after meals as generally people only used their fingers for eating. Forks did exist in the 13th and 14th

66

centuries but only for serving, not for eating. Forks for eating were first introduced into England in the 17th century and then the fashion took quite a while to catch on.

The aquamanile may have originated in the Near or Middle East and been introduced into Western Europe as a result of the crusades in the 12th century. Most of the aquamaniles which have survived take the form of lions, horses, dragons or griffins.

Discussion/ Practical activities

1. Begin by getting the children to draw jugs *before* they have seen this picture. Ask them to try to remember jugs they have seen or used. Their jugs may be simple milk/water jugs such as they might have at home. They should decorate their pictures from memory. Talk about the component features of a jug – container, spout, handle – and how these may differ.

2. Show the picture and ask what it is. Look for the distinguishing features that show the animal is a lion. Why is it a big fat dumpy lion? (Because it needs to hold a fair amount of liquid.) Why does it have a thin person on it? (Because it is a handle.) Notice the solid squat legs. Discuss how this aspect of the design allows the lion, and therefore its contents, to stand solidly without risk of spillage if it is knocked.

3. Look at the way the different parts of the jug are joined to each other. The person sitting on the lion has one leg up pushing against the lion while the other leg is firmly gripping the lion's flank. The two hands are clutching the lion's ears and this seems to have the effect of pulling the lion's head up. The balance and tension in this upright figure is supported by the arched handle which combines the tail of the lion with a mythical beast gripping the shoulders of the rider. Similarly the figure sliding in or out of the lion's mouth is gripping the lion's nose. Talk about the sense of fluid movement which reflects the movement of the liquid as it is poured. (There is no sense of tragedy here, although the figure is in the lion's mouth, it is more of a fun-fair ride.)

4. Discuss the square trap-door at the back of the lion's head which allows the container to be filled and the fact that liquid can be poured smoothly and steadily by simply lifting the back of the vessel while the animal remains standing on its front legs.

5. Now let the children get back to the drawing board and see if they have ideas to create their own extraordinary jugs. They can make three-dimensional models in clay and or other materials such as papier mâché.

6. Ask the children to design the matching bowl which almost certainly went with this aquamanile. It would be a bowl for washing hands in. They could also design a towel – to dry hands on!

7. Make a collection (objects and pictures) of unusual jugs and pots from a grandparent's cupboard, the local museum, or from books in the library.

Cross refer to other objects that are both decorative and functional: Palissy's dish (Picture 12), silver-gilt casket (Picture 1). Reference can also be made to objects in *Approaches to Art, Key Stage One*: Elephant and castle candlestick (Picture 28), pottery face-jug (Picture 29), Durham Cathedral knocker (Picture 40).

Picture 11

Avigdor Arikha (1929-): Scarlet Scarf on Studio Chair (1989).
Private collection; 81 x 61cm; oil on canvas.

AT1 main focus

POS: (i) *select and record images and ideas from first-hand observation*
(v) *apply their knowledge and experience of different materials, tools and techniques, using them experimentally and expressively*
(vi) *experiment with different qualities of line and tone in making images*
(ix) *experiment with ways of representing shape, form and space.*

Art topic work/cross curricular links

The activities suggested can form part of an art-focused topic on Observing and Responding; see page 23.

Background information

Avigdor Arikha is an Israeli artist born in 1929 and a survivor of the Nazi concentration camps. He lives and works in Paris. He draws and paints directly from life, producing work which comes from an astonishing clarity of perception. His paintings can be deceptively simple in appearance, but they seem to go right to the heart of the subject. A simple bag of potatoes, an alarm clock or a seated nude will each be approached with the same searching observation and humanity, so that we seem to be presented with the very essence of the subject.

Discussion/ Practical activities

1. Ask the children to make a simple pencil drawing of a chair before showing them this picture. Now show and talk about Arikha's picture. Why do the children think the artist painted it? Discuss the immediate shock of the colours, with the bright magenta scarf casually placed over the chair. Do the children think this is something the artist noticed and decided to paint, or was it arranged specially?

2. Discuss the angle from which the artist has painted the chair. Is it from the side or the front, for instance? Get the children to look at the

drawings they have made. Have they drawn the chair from the front or side? They may well have imagined the chair and drawn it sideways on. Talk about the way we imagine things and the way they *actually* look if we examine them very carefully. Here we are looking down at the chair from the back, a little to the right. So might the artist have been sitting or standing when he painted this picture? What is another reason for thinking that the artist was standing and looking down on the subject? (The floor takes up the whole area of the background.)

3.   The painting looks as if it has been made on a canvas which was given an overall red-brown **tone** before work began on the painting. This means that the artist has painted all the gaps between the chair legs, seat and scarf etc. as positive shapes using an **opaque** blue/grey/white colour. Discuss this with the children (i.e. that you don't have to paint the thing itself, but you can look at and draw or paint the shapes in between its various components).

4.   Talk about why the artist may have chosen to paint a magenta scarf rather than another coloured scarf. What does it make you think of? Is it a **warm** or **cold colour**? Why? (Refer to Picture 4 for more detailed discussion about warm and cold colours.)

5.   The chair is from the artist's studio. Does it look comfortable to sit on? Discuss the **design** of the chair with its long legs and curved back to give height and support – just what is required if you are sitting drawing or painting at an easel. This could also lead on to a discussion about chair design in general – different designs for different functions.

6.   Make some comparisons with other chairs in paintings, for example, Vincent van Gogh's 'Chair' in the National Gallery and his painting of 'Gauguin's Chair' in Amsterdam. Discuss how artists use their paint to describe the character of the chairs. Do chairs have personalities like people? Do different chairs suit different people?

Cross refer to the seats in Gainsborough's 'Mr and Mrs Andrews' (Picture 4) and Moore's 'King and Queen' (Picture 7).

7.   Make drawings and paintings from life using chairs, tables or stools as subjects. Find unusual angles to draw them from, so that what comes out is a response to something seen rather than something imagined.

Make a simple viewfinder to work out how a **composition** might fit best onto your paper: Cut a rectangular shape out of the middle of a piece of card to the scale of the paper you will be working on. Hold the viewfinder in front of your subject so that you can see how it might fit onto the paper. Use grey, black or coloured paper, so you can chalk in the shapes between the chair legs etc.

8.   Paint or draw your favourite chair, or an imaginary one. Perhaps one that provides you with refreshments, or includes some of your favourite things in it, or perhaps a magic chair which could transport you to different places.

9.   Write a poem or short story inspired by Arikha's painting.

Cross refer to other works of art produced from direct observation: Sargent's 'Carnation, Lily, Lily, Rose' (Picture 30), Cézanne's 'Pommes Vertes' (Picture 34) and Delacroix's 'Interior of Moroccan House' (Picture 29).

Picture 12

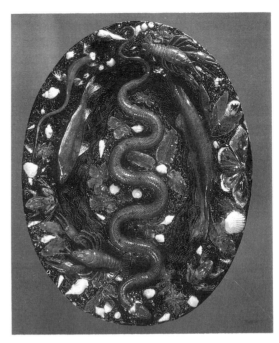

Bernard Palissy (c.1510-90): Oval dish with flora and fauna (1560).
British Museum, London; length: 52.3cm; moulded earthenware.

AT1 main focus

POS:
- **(ii)** *respond to memory and imagination using a range of media*
- **(iii)** *use a sketch-book to record observations and ideas*
- **(iv)** *experiment with ideas suggested by different source materials and explain how they have used them to develop their work*
- **(x)** *plan and make three-dimensional structures using various materials and for a variety of purposes*

Art topic work/cross curricular links

The activities suggested can form part of art-focused topics on Observing and Responding, Working in Three Dimensions and Art for a Purpose; see pages 23, 26 and 27.

Background information

Bernard Palissy first began making pottery at Saintes in France in 1542 and he continued there until 1565. In 1567 he set up a workshop situated in the grounds of the Palais des Tuileries in Paris, before the Royal Palace (the Louvre) was built. The area was used by many tile makers (*tuile* means tile) and other artisans.

Palissy's workshop was fairly large and some of the production processes may have been done by specialists. Palissy himself was very prolific but although he wrote many books and considered himself an expert and innovator in this field, there is not much information available today about his work. In fact his work is the subject of much controversy. Palissy's pottery became very popular during his lifetime and his style was copied by others. In the 19th century there was a revival of his work and **reproductions** of his original pieces were made.

The pottery Palissy produced was very different to any contemporary work and was characterised by figures and ornaments moulded in **relief**. **Moulds**, probably of plaster, would be made directly from real objects such as shells, leaves and dead creatures. They would then be attached to the main object, fired and covered with coloured **glazes** – mainly yellow, blue, green, brown and manganese. Finally, clear lead glazes would be applied.

This particular dish, which is typical of his fantastic flora and fauna pieces, is attributed to Palissy himself. It would probably have been used for decorative rather than practical purposes.

Discussion

1. First get the children to identify as many of the things on the dish as they can. What does the dish look like to them? A pond or river, for instance? Ask what it might be used for and if they would like to have their food served from such a plate. Would such a plate be easy or difficult to wash up?

2. Talk about the way the objects have been incorporated in the design. What effect does the eel snaking its way through the middle have on the overall look of the dish? Does it make it look cramped and busy or does it help make the surrounding space look larger? Is it the main focus of the dish?

Practical activities

1. Look at the decoration of your own household crockery. Do you have decorated dishes, vases, or figures at home? Look at the pots and dishes created by other cultures and try to find examples which incorporate a variety of images. Record these images in a sketch-book.

2. Use the images collected to design over-the-top dishes of your own, similar to the one by Palissy. Find themes for the dishes. These might be associated with on-going English or Science projects, or could be community-baseed themes. Try a number of designs before deciding on the one to make in clay. Or do this as a small team project, each member making a separate clay figure for one large dish.

Picture 13

Jan van Eyck (c.1390-1441): The Arnolfini Marriage, also known as Portrait of Giovanni Arnolfini (?) and Giovanna Cenami (?), (1434).
National Gallery, London; 87 x 52.4cm; oil on wood.

AT1 main focus

POS:
  (i) *select and record images and ideas from first-hand observation*
  (iv) *experiment with ideas suggested by different source materials and explain how they have used them to develop their work*
  (viii) *experiment with pattern and texture in designing and making images and artefacts*

Art topic work/cross curricular links

The activities suggested can form part of an art-focused topic on Portrait (see Images of Self and Family); see page 20.
The picture can also be used when focusing on using pictures as evidence in History; see page 30.

Background information

Jan van Eyck's outstanding skills ensured him an international reputation in the 15th century. He was based in Bruges and employed by the then ruler of the Netherlands, the Duke of Burgundy. He achieved an extraordinary illusion of reality in his paintings based on his careful observations of the play of light on a variety of surfaces. He perfected (but did not invent) a technique of **oil painting** which he applied in thin layers or **glazes** which enabled him to work up an astonishing degree of detail. Oil's slow drying time also made it possible to make changes more easily than with any other medium, for example **egg tempera.** (See picture 28, 'The Wish of Young Saint Francis'.) Changes or alterations can sometimes be seen, or they become more visible as the paint becomes more transparent with age, and are called **pentimenti**. (The singular form is pentimento, from the Italian *pentire* meaning to repent.) In this painting pentimenti are visible in the positions of the man's feet, his raised hand and the brush hanging on the wall.

It is the oil **medium** that has allowed van Eyck to achieve an extraordinary range of **tones**, with the deepest of shadows in transparent glaze colours (an effect that would be impossible in egg tempera) and the clarity of bright light in **opaque** colours on the face and head-dress of Giovanna Cenami. The oil medium also enables van Eyck to blend the paint. The resulting modulations in tone and colour, give a palpability to the light which touches every detail in the painting with the same gentleness that we see in the joined hands of the couple.

Van Eyck painted different types of pictures but most frequently altarpieces and **portraits**. The identity of the two people in this painting is not absolutely certain, hence the question marks in the title, but the most likely candidates are Giovanni Arnolfini and his wife Giovanna Cenami. In the earliest surviving document which seems to refer to this painting (a 16th-century inventory of the paintings in Margaret of Austria's collection), they are described as 'Hernoult le Fin' or 'Arnoult Fin' and his wife. It seems that at that time the painting was in a frame with **wings** (shutters) attached at either side on which identifying coats of arms could have been painted.

Giovanni Arnolfini was an Italian cloth merchant whose family and that of his wife came from Lucca, an important centre for woven textiles in Tuscany. Bruges, a flourishing centre for trade and commerce in the first half of the 15th century, enjoyed close ties with Italian towns and cities and became home for a large Italian community. Van Eyck lived and worked near the Spiegelrei or Quay of Mirrors, named after the mirror glass which was imported from Venice.

The clothes of the Arnolfinis and the objects which surround them indicate their wealth and status. This double portrait was probably commissioned to commemorate the couple's married state rather than their wedding ceremony. The main object which has prompted a range of interpretations is the lighted candle in the candelabra, since lighted candles were sometimes included in religious images. The scenes in the roundels on the mirror frame show the Passion of Christ. The glass beads hanging to the left of the mirror are rosary beads. The brush hanging from the tall chair back on the right seems to go with the carved figure of Saint Margaret (with her symbol the dragon), the patron saint of childbirth.

The Arnolfinis are fashionably dressed as might be expected. Giovanna conforms in every way to contemporary ideas of female beauty. These included swollen bellies emphasised by copious amounts of folded cloth – since female saints were also shown like this it is most unlikely that Giovanna Cenami is pregnant! (The inclusion of Saint Margaret does not imply an imminent new arrival either!)

Discussion

1. Tell the children to look closely at these two people.
   At what, or at whom, are the couple looking?
   Who is looking at them? (We are of course, but we might also think of the artist. Notice the two people reflected in the mirror – one in blue, the other in red. Perhaps one of them is the artist?)
   Do you think the dog has noticed them/us?
   Is the dog reflected in the mirror?
   Are there any other things which you can see in the room but which are not reflected in the mirror or vice-versa? The convex glass of the mirror distorts the reflection but also acts like a wide-angle lens so you can see quite a lot of the room in it.

2. Ask the children how they can tell this is a wealthy couple. Look for clues in their clothes – their style and the materials they are made of (his hat is beaver skin); the oranges, which were very expensive to import into Northern Europe at this time; the carpet on the floor (carpets were often put on tables and walls rather than floors); the candelabra and mirror.

3. Point out the wooden shoes in the **foreground** on the left which are pattens. Giovanni Arnolfini would have worn them outside to protect his soft leather boots from the dirt and mud in the streets. (This was long before pavements and tarmac roads; in fact pattens were still used well into the 19th century.) How can you tell these pattens have been used? Do you think the red shoes in the **background** are pattens? Who do you think these belong to?

4. Jan van Eyck signed the painting in a very fancy way above the mirror. It says '*Johannes de eyck fuit hic 1434*' which is Latin for 'Jan van Eyck was here 1434' (the year he painted the picture). Talk about why he put his name here in this way.

5. Ask the children what they think would have been the most difficult thing in the picture to paint and why.

6. Which colours particularly catch the eye? Consider the **complementary colours** here, for example Giovanna's green dress next to the red drapes of the bed. (Refer to Picture 30 for more detail about complementary colours.)

Practical activities

1. The painting shows a couple possibly celebrating their marriage. Look at the ways different cultures celebrate marriages or partnerships. Discuss your experiences of such occasions. Find photos and other material such as videos and then make your own images around this theme. Do some research into the couples back through the generations in your own family and if there is no visual material, make up some pictures based on what you have gathered about, for example, your great-grandparents. Your artwork could be two or three dimensional.

2. Practise drawing and painting from direct observation with particular attention to light, shadow and texture. Study objects with reflective surfaces, wood grain objects or hairy objects/animals.

3. Paint a portrait of yourself or a friend in a room which includes objects which give some clues about your/their interests. If you paint a picture of your friend can you work out a way of including yourself in the picture too, perhaps in a mirror or something similar?

4. Trace the template (on page 152) of van Eyck's signature to get a feel for this kind of writing. Then work out a design for your own signature. You might like to compare different scripts. This could develop into an exploration of **calligraphy**. (Refer to Picture 39, the *Luttrell Psalter*, for more details and activities about calligraphy.)

5. Find a convex mirror and do some drawings of the reflection(s) you can see. (Cross refer to Picture 14, Parmigianino's 'Self-portrait'.)

6. Since some people think the lighted candle is a candle clock, (although we don't because it's too high), used not only to tell the time but to seal legal agreements (i.e. once the candle had burned down any agreement made was binding), another possible activity would be to design and make a candle clock.

Cross refer to Gainsborough's 'Mr and Mrs Andrews' (Picture 4), Lippi's 'Portrait of a Man and Woman' (Picture 40), Vermeer's 'Kitchenmaid' (Picture 20).

Picture 14

Francesco Mazzola, known as 'Parmigianino' (1503-40): Self-Portrait in a Convex Mirror (1523-4).
Kunsthistorisches Museum, Vienna; diameter: 24.4cm; wooden roundel.

Picture 15

William Scrots (15-16th C.): Anamorphic Portrait of Edward VI (1546).
National Portrait Gallery, London; 42.5 x 160cm; painted wooden panel.

AT1 main focus

POS: **(i)** *select and record images and ideas from first-hand observation*
(v) *apply their knowledge and experience of different materials, tools and techniques, using them experimentally and expressively*
(ix) *experiment with ways of representing shape, form and space*

Art topic work/cross curricular links

The activities suggested can form part of art-focused topics on Portrait (see Images of Self and Family) and Transformations; see pages 20 and 25.
The picture can also be used when focusing on using pictures as evidence in History; see page 28.

Introductory note

These two images are about ideas of **perception**, how we get used to particular ways of seeing ourselves but how some very simple changes will radically alter these perceptions.

76

Parmigianino's self-portrait.

This picture shows a **distorted portrait.** It is the artist's **self-portrait** in a convex mirror painted on a convex wooden panel. He did it when he was about 20 years old.

His left hand projects forward, presumably to hold the paper he is drawing on with his right hand (which we cannot see), while the walls and the ceiling of the room he is in, curve curiously above him.

The artist was one of a number working in the mid to late 16th century, who are known as **Mannerists.** Their works often contain puzzling distortions of **proportion, scale** and colour.

(The artist's real name was Francesco Mazzola. 'Parmigianino', his nickname by which he is always known, derives from Parma – the town in Italy where he was born.)

Discussion

1.   Talk about mirrors that distort. Many children will have encountered these in amusement arcades and fairgrounds. You also find them in people's homes – decorative ones on the wall or mirrors that are used for shaving and/or make up. If possible, take such a mirror into the classroom.

2.   There is a decorative convex mirror in Picture 13 'The Arnolfini Marriage'. Bring this into the discussion too. Point out how a convex mirror can show more than a flat one – the whole room in the van Eyck is reflected, ceiling, floor, walls.

Practical activities

The activities you undertake here will depend upon what sort of distorting mirrors you can get hold of.

1.   Bring in shiny spoons (dessert size) and make images based on your distorted reflection from the convex surface. For this to work best, it is good to have your face in sunlight (coming in through a window for example), and with a dark background. This way you will be able to see the images more clearly and draw them more accurately.

2.   If larger distorting mirrored surfaces are available to you (for instance a Hall of Mirrors), do full scale self-portraits, drawing first and then using paints.

Anamorphic portrait of Edward VI.

This is an **anamorphic** portrait of Edward (the son of Henry VIII and Jane Seymour) painted in 1546, the year before he became king at the age of ten.

The image has been deliberately distorted. It is an anamorphosis which comes from the Greek word meaning 'transform'. The artist has used **perspective** in such a way that the image only looks 'right' when the picture is seen from the side. The original picture is painted on wood and there is a hole in the frame on the right-hand side so that you can see the image edge-on – at which point the perspective will seem more or less correct. You can get an idea of this by looking, in a similar manner, along the page of the book (put the edge of the book near your eye). The boy's face will then appear in a circle, with the words round the edge: *aetatis suae+9* – Latin for 'his age+9', and *ANo DNi+1546* – Latin short form of *Anno Domini*, 'in the year of our Lord – 1546'.

The circle is set against a **landscape background** which is meant to be seen from in front. This landscape is not original, it was added sometime in the 17th century. The picture was probably painted for the amusement of the young prince.

Anamorphic images were fashionable in the 16th century as were pictures with hidden symbolic or otherwise obscure meanings.

Scrots is a little-known artist who had been court painter to Mary of Hungary, Regent of the Netherlands. He came to England in 1545 and succeeded Holbein as painter to the King.

1.　Distortion of this type is done mathematically using a grid. You find this sort of thing still being done today. Road markings painted onto the road are done in perspective so that they do not seem at all distorted to the car drivers who see them at an angle as they drive along close to the road, but which look very elongated if seen from directly overhead.

2.　Here are some diagrams to show how these distortions are done:

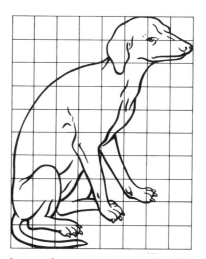

Image drawn onto squared grid.

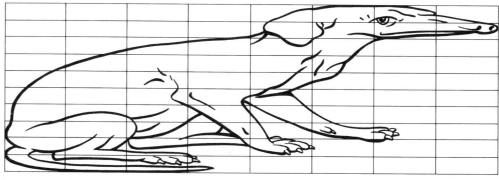

Image transferred onto rectangular grid.

3. Draw up your own anamorphic projection. (Use the template grids on pages 153 and 154). Choose a very simple image such as a flower or clock, and draw it onto the squared template. Then transfer the image, square by square, onto the rectangular template.

4. Bring in photographs of yourselves and draw a rectangular grid over them. Reproduce this grid in perspective (i.e. so that the sections are trapezoid), and copy the photograph square by square onto the new grid. You will end up with an anamorphic projection which looks crazy from face-on, but viewed from an oblique angle will look lifelike.

1. Talk about conventions of perspective and look at ways of depicting form and space according to different cultural traditions (i.e. how some cultures might show a simple object such as a chair from both sides and from the front at the same time).

Cross refer to two pictures in *Approaches to Art, Key Stage One*: Egyptian wall painting (Picture 26) and Hockney's 'Shoes Kyoto' (Picture 27).

2. Make some drawings in which you try to show in the same image absolutely everything you can see, including everything at the edges of your vision. Keep your eyes fixed ahead of you. The drawing will probably come out as circular.

Cross refer to pictures featuring other mirrors: van Eyck's 'Arnolfini Marriage' (Picture 13), *De Claris Mulieribus* (Picture 19).

Picture 16

John Constable (1776-1837): Cloud Study (A Skylark) (28.9.1821).
Yale Center for British Art, Paul Mellon Foundation New Haven, Conn.;
24.7 x 30.3cm; oil on paper on board.

Picture 17

John Constable (1776-1837): Cloud Study (25.9.1821).
Yale Center for British Art, Paul Mellon Foundation, New Haven, Conn.;
21.25 x 29cm; oil on paper on board.

AT1 main focus

POS: (i)   *select and record images and ideas from first-hand observation*
(iii)   *use a sketch-book to record observations and ideas*
(vi)   *experiment with different qualities of line and tone in making images*
(vii) *apply the principles of colour mixing in making various kinds of images*

Art topic work/cross curricular links

The activities suggested can form part of art-focused topics on Aspects of Landscape
and Observing and Responding; see pages 22 and 23.

John Constable was born at East Bergholt in Suffolk in 1776 and died in London in 1837. He was one of the great European landscape painters of whom it is said he began by being a good artist and by sheer force of will turned himself into a great one. Throughout his life, much of his work was based on an intense observation of nature, and his native landscape of Suffolk on the Essex borders, incorporating the Stour valley and Dedham Vale, became the focus for a rich body of work. He would paint the same scene many times in different weather conditions or from slightly different points of view, in an attempt to get to the heart of the subject and closer to the heart of painting itself.

Constable later moved to London and made paintings in Hampstead, Brighton and Salisbury. For many artists the great inspiration in Constable's work is in the intense, loose studies he made from nature rather than in the great 'set-piece' paintings. These studies were made during the period from 1819 to 1826, when the Constables rented a house at Hampstead during the summer months.

Discussion

1.   Talk about the types of skies that the children have seen and remembered. Go outside, look at the sky and talk about the cloud effects now and how they relate to the weather. Look at Constable's sketches and imagine what it would have been like to be outside on those days. What clues do the birds give as to what the weather is doing?

These cloud studies, and most of the others that Constable painted, are accompanied by inscriptions on the back which note the particular type of weather, often the time of day and other relevant information. The inscription on Picture 16 reads: 'Sep. 28 1821 Noon – looking North West, windy from the S.W. Large bright clouds flying rather fast. Very stormy night followed'.

2.   Look at the two sketches together. What are the main differences in the skies? Discuss the shapes of the clouds, the colours, lights, darks, sense of movement, birds etc.

3.   These sketches are quite small but ask the children what makes them seem bigger – as spacious as the sky. Do they think it has something to do with the fact that you cannot see any land, and the clouds fill the whole sketch?

4.   If you look closely you can see that the artist painted these clouds on dark paper. Can the children tell how he has brushed the paint on? Are all the strokes in the same direction? Are they all the same length? How would you describe them?

5.   Constable made these sketches outside. Talk about why he would have had to work quickly. Have the children ever painted clouds? Have they been easy or difficult to paint? Why?

6.   Look at the way clouds have been shown in other pictures. Cross refer here to photographs and paintings: Gainsborough's 'Mr and Mrs Andrews' (Picture 4), Moore's 'King and Queen' (Picture 7), Gilbert and George's 'Weather Window' (Picture 37), Martin's 'The Bard' (Picture 8), Lorraine's 'Embarkation of Saint Ursula' (Picture 24), Guercino's 'Aurora' (Picture 33), Efiaimbelo's 'Aloalo' (Picture 18), Bruegel's 'Fall of Icarus' (Picture 3).

 *Practical activities*

1.   Make cloud studies and write notes about them in the way that Constable did. A good way of being able to see clouds well is to wear sunglasses. This will enable you to see the shapes very clearly.

There are various ways of recording clouds. You can make rapid pencil sketches on white paper and work them up later as paintings. You can work with pastels or chalks on **toned** (coloured) paper. This is a good method because it allows you to work tonally, rubbing the pastel or chalk with your fingers or the palm of your hand to create fluffy edges and **tonal variations**. You can paint using thin **transparent** washes on white paper to make your cloud effects or you can paint with **opaque** colour mixed with white.

Efiaimbelo (1925-): Aloalo – Soroboko Avisoa in Mahafaly Land (1991-2).
The Jean Pigozzi Contemporary African Art Collection; 237 x 45 x 45cm; wood and acrylic.

AT1 main focus

POS: **(ii)** *respond to memory and imagination using a range of materials*
(iv) *experiment with ideas suggested by different source materials and explain how they have used them to develop their work*
(x) *plan and make three-dimensional structures using various materials and for a variety of purposes*

Art topic work/cross curricular links

The activities suggested can form part of art-focused topics on Working in Three Dimensions and Images of Self and Family; see pages 26 and 20.

Background information

This painted wooden sculpture is a contemporary funerary monument. It was made to celebrate the life of a particular individual, as well as the epoch in which he lived. It also follows a very traditional pattern of funerary art in Mahafaly society which has been passed down the generations from the beginning of the 16th century.

The technique uses sculptured poles (*alouals*) of a dark hardwood called mendorave. The lower part consists of eight (the number of completeness) layered motifs in alternate designs. Each design represents different myths and legends. The eighth motif is a full moon topped by a figurative scene carved **in the round**. The images portrayed in the scene may represent the profession of the deceased or refer to some relevant aspect of his or her life.

This particular monument shows a figure following a turtle or tortoise in the shade of a tree with spiky leaves, while an aeroplane passes overhead. The chunky clarity of this carved and painted wooden sculpture in which everything is so clearly expressed, allows one to ignore the pole on which the aeroplane sits, for example, and imagine the plane in mid-air.

Discussion

1.   This sculpture is made of painted wood. Talk about what catches your eye when you look at it and why. Why do the children think it was photographed at this angle? How tall do they think it is?

2.   The sculpture was made in the memory of a particular person. What does it tell us about the person?

3.   Discuss why the sculpture was painted in this way. The patterns on the pole follow a traditional design which was used for this kind of monument but how can one tell that the whole sculpture is quite new? (Think about the things in it, the appearance of the paint and the fact that it is outside.)

4.   Think about different ways of commemorating dead people. What kinds of monument can be found locally? What materials are used to make them? How long have they lasted? (This is particularly pertinent to cemeteries/graveyards and head stones.)

Practical activities

1.   Make similar sculptures using clay or balsa wood in which you set up simple scenes that focus on aspects of yourself that you consider important. Or take another individual whom you know, love or admire and use him or her as the basis for the work. The idea is to make a portrait without necessarily having to represent the person him or herself.

Cross refer to other artefacts and paintings with a functional purpose: bronze aquamanile (Picture 10), van Eyck's 'Arnolfini Marriage' (Picture 13) and the Lewis Chessmen (Picture 35).

Picture 19

French (14-15th C.): page from Boccaccio's *De Claris Mulieribus* showing a women painting a self-portrait using a mirror (1402).
Bibliothèque Nationale, Paris; 8 x 6.5cm; illuminated manuscript.

AT1 main focus

POS: (i) *select and record images and ideas from first-hand observation*
(v) *apply their knowledge and experience of different materials, tools and techniques, using them experimentally and expressively*
(vi) *experiment with different qualities of line and tone in making images*

Art topic work/cross curricular links

The activities suggested can form part of art-focused topics on Images of Self and Family and Observing and Responding; see pages 20 and 23.

Background information

De Claris Mulierbus (*On Famous Women*) was written by the Italian Boccaccio, in the 14th century. This picture comes from a copy of the work made in France in the early 15th century.

This **illumination** is of Marcia, a celebrated lady painter from the Ancient World. Boccaccio would have read about her in Pliny's work*.

The 15th-century French illuminator has depicted Marcia in a contemporary dress and setting. She is shown at work on a **self-portrait**. She holds a small hand mirror, in which we see her face reflected as she paints her head and shoulders on a panel which is propped on the work-bench in front of her. She has a small **palette** and some brushes nearby.

On a bench to her left, further equipment is laid out. We can see a box and various pots and dishes containing different colours. It was common practice to put prepared colour into shells and the yellow **ochre** paint may well be in a mussel shell.

85

The furniture shown here is grand for this period and both floor and walls are tiled. This is very much the dwelling or work place of someone prosperous.

Much of our knowledge of the techniques used by painters of this period comes from a famous treatise, *The Craftsman's Handbook*, written in the late 14th century by the Italian Cennino Cennini. (A modern translation is available in paperback, published by Dover.)

The panel on which Marcia is shown working, would – if it were real – probably be oak if the artist was from Northern Europe, or poplar if Italian. (Canvas as a **support** for painting started to be used seriously in the late 15th century.) Artists had to make their own paint at this time. It involved grinding up powdered **pigment**. Then a sticky substance (the **medium**) was added to make the colour adhere to the panel. At this time the most common medium for panel painting was egg yolk. The best brushes were made with hog-bristles or minever (ermine) hair. Cennino Cennini describes how to make brushes from the ermine's tail hairs by cooking them and setting them into a quill.

There were many stages in the preparation of the panel before painting took place. (See page 87 for a detailed description.)

* Pliny the Elder, A.D. 23-79, is very important for the tradition and diffusion of Western culture. He is known to have written seven books of which only one survives – *Natural History* – which gives a clear indication of the state of scientific knowledge in 1st century Rome. It was a work much admired by scholars in the Middle Ages. Pliny died while watching the eruption of the famous volcano, Vesuvius, which engulfed Pompeii!

Discussion

1.   Ask the children what this lady is doing. What sort of picture is she painting? (A self-portrait.) Talk about paint (that it consists of pigment and medium). What shape is the palette and what is it used for? What were brushes made of?

2.   Encourage the children to describe her clothes and hairstyle. Discuss the room she is in and the furniture you can see.

3.   Talk about the portrait she is painting. Introduce terms such as **full face, three-quarter view** and **profile**.

Practical activities

1.   Painting self-portraits. To do this mirrors are required. (Mirror tiles can be useful here as they often come with a self-adhesive back and can be fixed to a wall or notice-board. But beware – these can cause damage to the wall when removed!)

Before painting you will need to *draw* your self-portrait. In the early Renaissance the artists would have sketched it in with charcoal, then rubbed the charcoal off with chicken feathers. (Use a soft dry brush today.) This would leave a residual image which would be drawn in more finely using a small brush and *very* diluted ink. They would then start the painting process. Do yours in the same way.

Decide whether to paint just a face or head and shoulders. What can you see in the mirror? You may elect to just paint part of your face – one side of it perhaps. Draw lightly at first to get the **proportions** about right. Before starting, look carefully at the reflection and think about what you can see. Discuss the colour(s) of the skin, **highlights** and **shading**. Talk about the eye – what is it that makes it appear shiny? Discuss the proportion. How far apart are the eyes and how far up the face are they? (Use phrases like 'more than half' if the children are not familiar with thirds, etc.)

2.   Another approach which you could consider is for the children to work in pairs. One to work on a self-portrait as above, while the other works on a picture of his/her partner painting the self-portrait.

3.   As a special painting project which is fun to do and not too difficult, you can work using early **Renaissance** methods:

i)   Begin by making **gesso** panels. Cut some fairly small pieces of hardboard and give them a coat (front, back and sides) of glue size, (70 grams rabbit-skin glue per litre of water), and let it dry.

ii)   Mix the warm glue size solution with plaster of Paris or chalk to a creamy consistency and apply to the panel with a stiff brush. Brush some onto the edges and the back of the panel as well, to prevent the panel from bowing.

iii)   Keep adding layers as it dries so there is a good coat of gesso on the panel. When this is completely dry, sand to a smooth finish.

iv)   To prepare egg **tempera** paints, you will need pigments (use standard powder colour), water (preferably distilled but this is not essential), and egg yolk. (To produce egg yolk, crack the egg carefully and let the unbroken yolk sac roll around on a piece of kitchen towel to rid it of the egg white. Then puncture it so that the yolk runs into a jar.) Mix the powder with a little water and add a little egg yolk. This is egg tempera paint and similar to that used by the early Renaissance painters.

v)   Apply the paint to the gesso panel with a round pointed soft-hair brush using hatching strokes (i.e. fine, closely set parallel lines).

Cross refer to other women artists: Morisot (Picture 25) and Ayres (Picture 41).

Cross refer to the use of egg tempera in Sassetta's 'The Wish of Young Saint Francis' (Picture 38).

Picture 20

Johannes (Jan) Vermeer (1632-75): The Kitchenmaid (1658).
Rijksmuseum, Amsterdam; 45.5 x 44cm; oil on canvas.

AT1 main focus

POS: **(ii)** *respond to memory and imagination using a range of media*
(vii) *apply the principles of colour mixing in making various kinds of images*

Art topic work/cross curricular links

The activities suggested can form part of an art-focused topic on Images of Self and Family; see page 20.
The picture can also be used when focusing on using pictures as evidence in History; see page 28.

Background information

In the time of Vermeer, the country we now often call Holland consisted of seven provinces, each with large towns and local schools of painting. During this period there was an enormous increase in artistic activity. There are a number of reasons for this, one of which was an increase in middle-class affluence which led to a demand for paintings. People wanted fairly small-scale paintings, of a size which would look good in their houses. They particularly liked pictures of local, everyday subject matter, such as the local **landscape** or street scenes, domestic interiors, **portraits** of themselves and their families and so on.

At this time a large number of painters became specialists in one **genre** or another, and instead of painting pictures to order, produced them speculatively and sold them through art dealers who now emerged for the first time. Many artists found it difficult to make a living in this way and had to have other jobs as well to supplement their incomes.

Johannes (or Jan) Vermeer was one of these painters and nowadays he is considered to be one of the very best. He lived and worked in Delft, a town which had become prosperous largely due to majolica factories and breweries. Not very much is known about Vermeer, but it is known that he worked as an art dealer and when he died at the age of 43 he left a widow, eleven children and debts.

Only a few (about 30) paintings by Vermeer are known, possibly because his meticulous style meant that he worked very slowly.

This quiet domestic scene of a woman in a kitchen was painted in 1658. The woman's clothes, the style of the room and the objects in it are all contemporary. The box on the floor is a foot warmer consisting of a wooden box with a perforated top into which you put an earthenware pot of glowing embers. We think the basket on the wall might be a bread basket and that the polished brass container next to it might be for carrying hot things.

The window is glazed with small panes of glass – large panes were still hard to make at this time, so almost all domestic windows were made this way, with small panes joined by lead strips. The light in the picture pours in through this window, raking across the woman and the objects in the room. Look at the rim of the milk-jug and the way the light plays on the other pots and on the crusty surface of the bread.

There is an extraordinary sense of the present moment in this painting. As viewers, we have a sense of being there, of almost participating in the scene. This makes it very different from many of the other portraits in this book in which we may admire the sumptuousness of their clothes or jewellery but we maintain a certain distance. The painting is what it is, a study of a woman pouring milk. Her sleeves are rolled up because she is engaged in household work. Her dress is simple. The painting has the quality of transforming something quite ordinary into a special quiet moment. We do not know what the woman is thinking but she has a poise and grace which seems to arise out of her concentration and focus on the task.

Discussion

1.   Talk about what can be seen *in* the painting. Why is the table by the window? What sort of artificial lighting was available to people at this time? Why would people need footwarmers like that? How do we keep warm nowadays? (The long skirts and hats worn in those days would also have related to keeping warm.)

Talk about Vermeer's meticulous attention to detail: the nail in the back wall for example, the weave of the baskets and the shine on the pots, even the stitching on the woman's dress is minutely observed and recorded.

2.   Now discuss what the artist has *left out*, because with this painting in particular a lot of its strength and power is due to the artist having been very selective. For example, discuss the colours he has used. There are a few very strong ones – that eye-catching yellow and the blue of the apron repeated in the cloth on the table. The rich red of the skirt and the dark green of the tablecloth. All are simple strong clear colours set off by the cool grey plaster wall behind the woman. The artist has used one green, one red, one blue and one yellow. There is no pattern in the fabrics' weave and no decoration on the wall (except the minimal tiles).

Vermeer could have put shelves on the walls, a view through the window, a cat or mouse on the floor. He could have shown us more of the room, the woman's feet even, or the ceiling, a vista through a door into a room beyond. But he didn't. Choosing what to put in and what to leave out is part of what making a successful picture is all about.

Practical activities

1.   Paint a modern version of this picture. Just a table, a window and one person at work using a few things on the table. These days it is as likely to be a man as a woman who is cooking the family meal. Base your picture on the Vermeer. The paper should be almost square. The window (a modern one) and the table should be in the same position and the figure should likewise be positioned similarly and take up the same proportion of the picture surface. Limit the colours and limit the amount of clutter you put in.

2.   Extend Vermeer's picture by using the line sketch of the main figure and objects (see the template on page 155). Draw in some more of the room – what Vermeer chose to leave out!

Compare the 'Kitchenmaid' to the woman depicted by Filippo Lippi (Picture 40), the Indian figures (Picture 9) and to Vuillard's 'Woman in Blue with a Child' (Picture 2).

Picture 21

Manuel Jimenez (c.1925-); Wood Animals (1960).
Work no longer in existence; maximum height of any animal 20cm; paint on wood.

AT1 main focus

POS: **(ii)** *respond to memory and imagination using a range of materials*
(x) *plan and make three-dimensional structures using various materials and for a variety of purposes*

Art topic work/cross curricular links

The activities suggested can form part of an art-focused topic on Working in Three Dimensions; see page 26.

Background information

Manuel Jimenez is a Mexican folk artist from Oaxaca whose carvings of animals have an appealing quality of directness. They are alert and engaging but with an attraction that goes beyond the merely whimsical. These are works that arise from a deep understanding and love of animals based on observation and experience. The curve of a neck, the angle of a head, the position of a tail; all these fine and gentle touches combine to tell a story and to breathe life and character into the carvings. The bright fluorescent colours add to the energy and charge that seems contained within the carvings.

Unfortunately these particular animals have been destroyed by wood-boring beetles.

Discussion

1. Ask the children whether they think these carvings are based on real animals. If so, why? What kinds of animals might they be based on? Have they ever seen animals this colour? Why do you think the artist painted them like this? Some of these animals look as if they are asking questions. What kinds of questions might they be? (Anyone with a dog will know the 'Isn't it time you took me for a walk ?' look.)

2. Discuss how the animals may have been made.

3.   Talk about the limited number of colours the artist has used. (No blue/green/purple/brown etc.) Point out the use of lots of spots, but no stripes.

4.   Which one do the children like best, and why? Ask them to think up a name for their favourite. Do the children think they come out during the day or at night? What do animals like this eat?

Practical activities

1.   Whittling away at wood is not something we should perhaps ask Key Stage Two children to do. But they can carve other materials such as some of the foam blocks currently available and which only require blunt tools to be carved successfully.

2.   Alternatively, make three-dimensional models out of modelling materials such as Das and Fimo. If these are too expensive Plasticine and normal clay can be used, although the latter is rather brittle when dry, unless fired.

Each child should make one animal so that there could be a class collection of them. Decide on the scale – do you want them all to be about the same size? Think about the colour range – do you want to limit this, as in the illustration, or allow a free hand?

As the children work, discuss with them how to give their animal a character. The character of Jimenez's animals comes not just from the painted expression on the face, but from the angle of the head, the set of the ears and tail, and apparent body movement. Ask the children that have pets to concentrate on the qualities that they find endearing about them.

3.   Make up names and stories for some of Jimenez's animals.

Picture 22

William Blake (1757-1827): The Tyger from *Songs of Innocence and Experience* **(1794).**
Rosenwald Collection, Rare Book and Special Collections Division, Library of Congress, Washington; 18 x 12cm (whole page), 11 x 7cm (etching); relief etching.

AT1 main focus

POS: (ii) *respond to memory and imagination using a range of media*
(v) *apply their knowledge and experience of different materials, tools and techniques using them experimentally and expressively*
(vi) *experiment with different qualities of line and tone in making images*

Art topic work/cross curricular links

The activities suggested can form part of an art-focused topic on Imagination and Invention; see page 24.
The picture can also be used as a stimulus for work on manuscripts and presentation and imaginative writing; see pages 30, 31 and 32.

Background information

William Blake was an unconventional English artist, poet and philosopher. In his art he was sometimes very experimental, for example he would try out new techniques which did not always last very well, and consequently the condition of a number of his pictures has deteriorated severely.

Blake believed that the real visible world of the senses is like a cover behind which spiritual reality is concealed. His art work and his philosophical beliefs are very closely connected and both are sometimes quite hard to understand.

He was a very able poet and perhaps his most well known poetical work today is a section from his poem *Milton*. This section known as 'Jerusalem' was set to music by Parry and is traditionally sung by the Women's Institute and some secondary schools.

Blake brought his art and poetry together in what he called 'illuminated printing'. He wrote out his poems and drew in the surrounding designs. Then he **etched** and **printed** each page and when he had a purchaser would colour each one by hand. He wrote the collection of poems called *Song of Innocence* in 1788 and followed it up with *Songs of Experience* in 1794. They were issued in a single volume showing, as he put on the title page, 'the two Contrary States of the Human Soul'.

'The Tyger' comes from the *Songs of Experience*. The poem, reproduced here to make it easier to read, speculates on the nature of the power or deity which invented the tiger through a series of questions, none of which are answered. Above all it presents us with the problem of how to reconcile good and evil. It is, however, a mistake to try to dissect the meaning of this poem too much. This is impossible, and to try to do so will spoil the poem's completeness.

The Tiger

Tiger, tiger, burning bright
In the forests of the night,
What immortal hand or eye
Could frame thy fearful symmetry?

In what distant deeps or skies
Burnt the fire of thine eyes?
On what wings dare he aspire?
What the hand, dare seize the fire?

And what shoulder and what art
Could twist the sinews of thy heart?
And when thy heart began to beat,
What dread hand? And what dread feet?

What the hammer? What the chain?
In what furnace was thy brain?
What the anvil? What dread grasp?
Dare its deadly terrors clasp?

When the stars threw down their spears
And watered Heaven with their tears,
Did he smile his work to see?
Did he who made the lamb make thee?

Tiger, tiger, burning bright
In the forests of the night,
What immortal hand or eye
Dare frame thy fearful symmetry?

The actual page size of the original poem/illustration is just over 18cm by 12cm. The illustration itself is just under 11cm by 7cm, so in original copies it appears small, in the middle of the page, and with wide margins all round it.

Discussion

1.   The poem itself should be read aloud and discussed. Depending on the age of the children, you could get them to learn (at least part of) it by heart.

2. Explain to the children that this is a handwritten poem, where the handwriting has been printed, rather than **typeset**. The handwriting and the illustration form an integrated whole. The tree branches extend across the page sometimes forming wavy lines between the verses of the poem.

3. Talk about the tiger. Has Blake made it look frightening? Has he shown its **symmetry**? (Compare William Morris's work on symmetry on page 109.) In what way is a tiger symmetrical? In what way is the poem symmetrical? (The first and last verses are almost identical.) Has Blake shown the tiger 'in the forests of the night'?

4. Discuss the handwriting. Look at the curly capital letters and the way of making the 'G' in 'Tyger'. Talk about making a page attractive both in detail and as a whole.

Practical activities

This illustrated poem, and the *Luttrell Psalter* (Picture 39), can be used to explore the relationship between word and image. This is a fundamental aspect of children's development and especially so at Key Stage Two when the relationship becomes more complex and when children begin to illustrate particular concepts deriving either from an image created or from a phrase conceived.

1. Make up a short poem (we suggest a minimum of four lines) to be handwritten on an illuminated page. This will work well only if the task is well structured. First choose a topic to write about , e.g. an animal or flower, and then think at an early stage how to integrate the poem and illustration on the page. Make sure that you plan the page. Make faint pencil lines (which can be rubbed out later) for the text of the poem and make sure these lines are placed appropriately on the page. Write the poem in neat handwriting and illuminate the page with relevant artwork.

2. A simpler alternative would be to first draw the shape of the animal, and then compose the poetry to fit into that shape. However, the poetry will obviously be more limited.

3. Look at the section on William Morris and symmetry on page 109. Using the ink blot activity idea, make symmetrical tigers in the same way. (If possible, show the children pictures of tiger rugs which display the basic symmetry of tiger markings.) Give the children *half* a tiger to copy in *wet* ink, or paint along the fold in a plain piece of paper (some skill is needed here or you will get a black panther or worse). Use the template on page 156 for guidance. Fold the page and you should get a fearfully symmetrical tiger!

Cross refer to the illuminated page of the *Luttrell Psalter* (Picture 39) and the illustrated poem – Martin's 'The Bard' (Picture 8).

Cross refer to Rousseau's 'Tropical Storm with a Tiger' in *Approaches to Art, Key Stage One*.

Picture 23

Caspar David Friedrich (1774-1840): Two Men Contemplating the Moon (1819).
Gemaldergalerie Neue Meister, Dresden; 35 x 44.5cm; oil on canvas.

AT1 main focus

POS: (i)   *select and record images and ideas from first-hand observation*
(ii) *respond to memory and imagination using a range of media*
(vi) *experiment with different qualities of line and tone in making images*
(vii) *apply the principles of colour mixing in making various kinds of images*

Art topic work/cross curricular links

The activities suggested can form part of art-focused topics on Telling a Story and Aspects of Landscape; see pages 21 and 22.
The picture can also be used as a stimulus for creative writing; see page 32.

This curiously eerie scene was painted by the German artist Friedrich (pronounced Freed-rik) in 1819. He was an artist who was fond of painting evocative, mystical **landscapes** which often contained hidden meanings. He sometimes included himself in these pictures, gazing out into the distance. It is generally agreed that it is likely that the figure on the right in this picture is Friedrich himself, and the younger man on the left who leans on him is one of his pupils. They wear clothes which are similar to traditional German dress which had been revived during the War of Liberation (1813-15) and which had since been regarded as the costume of the democratic movement. It is, however, unlikely that any real political statement is being made here.

The picture has been interpreted in various ways, one of which is that the stony path along which the men walk may represent the path of life and the new waxing moon which illuminates this path is a symbol of Christ. The two men gaze out from the rough stony world of dead and dying trees at the infinity of space and the mysteries of the universe. (Note, a waxing moon is one which is growing – indeed, in the picture the entire form of the moon can be seen in ghostly shape. The bright 'star' nearby is likely to be one of the planets, probably Venus.)

Friedrich painted several versions of this picture and in one of these there is a man and a woman instead of two men.

Discussion

1.   Encourage the children to look closely at the picture, and to describe what they see. Where are the two men? What is the countryside like? What time of year is it? What time of the day is it? What is the path like? What are the men looking at? How would the children describe the trees? Do they think the rock formations are natural or man-made? Which man is older? Describe their clothes. Describe the colour of this picture. Have the children ever seen the moon looking like this?

2.   Point out how the oak tree is **silhouetted** against the sky. What makes the tree spooky? (Get the children to use vocabulary in an interesting way – introduce words such as 'twisted' and 'gnarled'.)

Practical activities

1.   Make some silhouette pictures by cutting the silhouettes out of black paper or card and sticking them onto an appropriate background (e.g. deep blue for the night sky). Base the silhouettes on things seen: trees, buildings, railings, people, animals etc. When the evenings are short the class can go to an area and make drawings of things they see silhouetted. Or create imaginary silhouettes of goblins, witches, fairies, gods and goddesses etc.

2.   Make a picture of a landscape using strips of differently shaded paper. Place the strips in order of **tone**, i.e. each getting lighter towards the back. Make some expressive shadow puppets, like the Javanese ones, and produce a short play.

3.   Talk about the possible symbolism of the path of life. If you were going to do a picture of the path of life how would you make it? Talk about symbols of birth (e.g. eggs hatching) and death (e.g. candles snuffed out).

Think up likely milestones in your life including birth and death and draw a path of life for yourself. Will your path be rough and stony, or smooth and flat?

4.   Make up a conversation that the two men in the picture might be having. Do you think they would be talking about the moon?

5.   Decide which colours you think convey a sombre, eerie mood and then try to produce them by experimenting with different colour mixes. When you have produced the colours you want, use them as backgrounds for silhouette pictures.

6.   What sort of creatures do you think live in Friedrich's landscape? Invent one. Decide where it lives. In the trees? Under a boulder? Is it camouflaged or does it have warning colouration?

Follow up

1.   Look at some examples of Jan Pieńkowski's work – he is a children's author and illustrator who frequently uses silhouettes in his books. *Christmas* and *Easter* contain particularly effective silhouettes of people and trees. Try to create similar spooky silhouettes and paste them onto marbled paper.

Cross refer to other depictions of the moon, stars, sun etc: Miró's 'The Red Sun' (Picture 32), Lorraine's 'Seaport' (Picture 24), Breugel's 'Fall of Icarus' (Picture 3) and Sassetta's 'Wish of Young Saint Francis' (Picture 38).

Picture 24

Claude Lorraine (1600-82): Seaport with the Embarkation of Saint Ursula (1641).
National Gallery, London; 148.6 x 193.7cm; oil on canvas.

AT1 main focus

POS: **(i)** *select and record images and ideas from first-hand observation*
(ii) *respond to memory and the imagination*
(ix) *experiment with ways of representing shape, form and space*
(x) *plan and make three-dimensional structures using various materials and for a variety of purposes*

Art topic work/cross curricular links

This painting can be discussed as part of a history/thematic work on ships and seafaring.

Claude Gellée was born in the Duchy of Lorraine (now part of France: Alsace-Lorraine), and was later to be known as Claude Lorraine. His interest in painting prompted him to go to Rome where he settled and became one of the most influential **landscape** painters of his generation. His ideal scenes, a combination of observed light effects and imagination, evoked a past Golden Age, associated with classical antiquity.

The subjects of his paintings were usually taken from classical literature such as Ovid's *Metamorphoses* or Virgil's *Aeneid*, but also included biblical themes and other religious narratives as here. He used these subjects as a vehicle for composing idyllic landscapes and seaports, since the painting of a landscape or **seascape** as a subject in its own right was taken less seriously by his contemporaries. He helped to change attitudes, however, and inspired many artists including two of the most famous British painters of the 19th century – Turner and Constable.

The appeal of the idealised settings he created was such that many British aristocrats of the 18th century (many of whom travelled to Rome on the Grand Tour as part of their education) had their country estates 'landscaped' in emulation of Lorraine's paintings, complete with classical temples!

One of the most daring innovations which Lorraine made was to include the sun, the brightest source of light, in his scenes, rather than suggest its presence off the picture to the left or right as previous artists had done. This enabled him to explore a range of dramatic and spatial light effects, especially when expanses of water were included.

'Seaport with the Embarkation of Saint Ursula' was painted for Fausti Poli one of the Pope's administrators and like many of Lorraine's pictures was one of a pair. Its partner was a 'Landscape with Saint George and the Dragon'.

Several versions of the story of Saint Ursula evolved including one in the *Golden Legend* (a 13th-century compilation of Saints' lives by Jacobus da Voragine). According to this version Ursula was the daughter of a Christian king of Brittany. She agreed to marry the son of a pagan English king provided that the prince was baptised a Christian and accompanied her on a pilgrimage to Rome. (The prince is not included in Lorraine's picture.) In one of the earliest versions of Ursula's legend she was to be accompanied on this pilgrimage by ten virgin attendants but by the time of the *Golden Legend* this number had increased dramatically to eleven thousand (possibly due to an earlier mistranscription)! On their return from Rome they stopped at Cologne where they were massacred by Huns and later declared to be martyrs. Lorraine met the challenge of representing Ursula with 11,000 companions without upsetting the balance and harmony of his composition by showing a fair number processing out of the building on the extreme left. We can imagine that the others are still inside. They seem to be carrying bows, an allusion to Ursula's future martyrdom by a Hun's arrow.

Discussion

1. Ask the children what preparations they can see being made for a sea voyage here? What is happening in the **foreground**? What is happening in the **background**? What time of day is this? (Consider at what time of day travellers usually set off; the position of sun and the early morning light.)

2. Talk about what seems to happen to the appearance of things as you look from the foreground to the background. Note how they get smaller, lighter and fainter, which helps create a sense of space.

Lorraine like many artists used laws of **perspective** to create illusions of space and depth in pictures. He applied **linear perspective** when painting the buildings and paved areas: receding lines if extended would converge at a vanishing point on the horizon. He applied **aerial perspective** to suggest depth and distance: imitating the effect of atmosphere on colours – they appear lighter and cooler in the distance.

3. Lorraine painted one of the ships right in the centre of the picture. Can the children spot it? (If you divided the picture into two halves – left and right – the dividing line would coincide with the ship's tallest mast.) What else helps draw our attention to this ship? (Note the light right behind it, the shadow in front of it, the direction of the quayside, the ropes, and the other ships/boats.)

4. Talk about how the passengers are to be ferried to the big ships. The most important person who is going on this journey is Saint Ursula, a princess. Discuss how the artist has made her stand out from

the friends who are travelling with her. Consider her size, the flag she's holding, her position in the picture, the colour of her dress, and her servant holding the train of her dress. What else is painted in the same colour as Saint Ursula's dress? Ask the children which three colours seem to be used the most. Is it accidental that these are the **primary colours**?

5. Encourage the children to describe the depiction of the sea. Talk about how the artist has suggested the swell of the sea. Compare this with other paintings of sea or water, such as: Hokusai's 'A Wild Sea at Chōshi' (Picture 26), Morisot's 'Summer's Day' (Picture 25), Bruegel's 'Fall of Icarus' (Picture 3) and Turner's 'Sunset' (Picture 16 in *Approaches to Art, Key Stage One*).

6. Explain that although this is an imaginary seaport, some of the ideas for it were based on the artist's sketches of natural effects and other things in real life. What sort of things do the children think he could have observed which would be useful for this picture?

Practical activities

1. Paint a watery picture based on sketches made from direct observation of light on water and after discussing different ways of painting water.

2. Paint a partner for this picture – perhaps your own version of a landscape with Saint George and the Dragon or another theme which would make a good contrast with this one.

3. Consider the differences between sea travel when Lorraine painted this picture and sea travel now. Make a picture of a sea journey real or imaginary.

4. Make a three-dimensional **diorama** like a model for a stage set, based on this scene. Make the image out of flat cardboard cut-outs painted realistically. Make sure you get the scale of each part right so that it looks realistic when you look at it from the front.

Follow up

1. Look at the design of ships/boats over centuries and find out what it was like to travel in them. Who would want to be where and what jobs would they have to do? (Who would volunteer to be look-out in the crow's nest?)

Picture 25

Berthe Morisot (1841-95): Summer's Day (c.1879).
National Gallery, London; 45.7 x 75.2cm; oil on canvas.

AT1 main focus

POS: **(i)** *select and record images and ideas from first-hand observation*
(iii) *use a sketch-book to record observations and ideas*
(iv) *apply the principles of colour mixing*
(viii) *experiment with pattern and texture in designing and making various kinds of images*

Art topic work/cross curricular links

The activities suggested can form part of art-focused topics on Aspects of Landscape and Observing and Responding; see pages 22 and 23. The picture can also be used as a stimulus for creative writing.

Background information

Berthe Morisot was fortunate to have been born into a wealthy and supportive family. Her parents were happy to encourage their daughter's active interest in painting. There was still considerable opposition in the 19th century to women artists, partly due to the emphasis placed on **life drawing** (i.e. studying the nude model) in academic art training, and partly due to attitudes against women pursuing any profession.

Berthe Morisot followed the recommendations of established painters, making copies of **Old Masters** in the Louvre and studying the effects of light in nature through sketches made out-of-doors. Such sketches were then used as the basis for **landscape** paintings worked up in the artist's studio. Some of Berthe Morisot's landscapes were accepted for exhibition in the Salon (the official annual exhibition in Paris) of 1864. She became increasingly interested in painting directly from life, working quickly to capture fleeting effects of light and began to exhibit her work independently from the Salon, with like-minded artists. These artists formed the basis of a new movement whose attention to modern life subjects and the techniques they used to convey the immediacy of a scene caused their critics to label them **'Impressionists'**.

The Impressionists were able to take advantage of modern manufactured **pigments** which dramatically extended the range of colours available to painters. The brilliance and stability (i.e. resistance to fading) of manufactured colours was an added advantage. The advent of metal tubes to contain the colours (pig bladders had been used before!) and a wider range of portable equipment made painting outside even easier. Canvases could also be bought in standard sizes ready-**primed** for oil painting. Berthe Morisot used such a canvas for this painting.

'Summer's Day' was exhibited at the fifth Impressionist exhibition in 1880 with a different title: 'The Lake in the Bois de Boulogne'. This was a favourite venue for the artist and she often painted scenes from boats on the lake. She used her sisters and other family members and friends as models. She in turn modelled for her brother-in-law, Edouard Manet; she had married his brother Eugène in 1874, the year of the first Impressionist exhibition. (There were eight Impressionist exhibitions: 1874, 1876, 1877, 1879, 1880, 1881, 1882 and 1886.)

Discussion

1. Talk about this painting. Ask the children whether they think that 'Summer's Day' is a good title for this picture. Encourage them to explain their answers. Discuss in which directions the two girls in the boat are looking. Where do you think the artist would be to get this view? How close do you think she was to the two girls? Does the boat look as though it is moving? If so, which way? Are the girls wearing the same kind of clothes that are worn today? What are the main differences between their summer clothes and our summer clothes? Are those umbrellas or parasols?

2. Talk about how the artist has painted the girls. Is it in great detail? How has she made their dress material look light and soft? Does it look shimmery like the water? How has she made the water look like water?

3. How many different colours has the artist used to paint the water? Where can you find touches of **warm colour**? (Refer to Picture 4 for more detailed discussion about warm and **cool colours**.) How many ducks can you see and what makes them stand out? What can you see at the far side of the lake?

4. Can you tell where the paint has been put on thinly and where thickly? Point out the different ways the artist used her paint brushes: long strokes, short strokes, quick dabs, zigzag sweeps. Are all the strokes going in the same direction? Do the children think she painted this quickly or slowly? How can they tell? Where has the artist put her name? Do the children think the picture is finished?

Practical activities

1. Paint a picture with the title 'Summer's Day'. Choose predominantly cool colours or warm colours to create the mood of the painting.

2. Paint an impression of your friend(s). See if you can describe what they look like quite quickly (before they change position!). Use the brushstrokes to suggest the texture and character of their hair and clothes.

3. Look carefully at the frothy brushwork the artist has used. Try something similar yourself.

4. If possible make some sketches of a stretch of water (pool, pond, lake) near your school or home. Use coloured pastels instead of paint to capture the appearance of the water: take care over the colours you use and the way you suggest light, reflections and movement over or in the water. Use your sketch as the basis for a painting back at school. Compare this painting with other watery pictures and themes: Hokusai's 'Wild Sea at Chōshi' (Picture 26), Bruegel's 'Fall of Icarus' (Picture 3), Lorraine's 'Embarkation of Saint Ursula' (Picture 24), and Palissy's oval dish (Picture 12).

Cross refer to pictures of light and materials/outdoor sketches/painterly pictures: Gainsborough's 'Mr and Mrs Andrews' (Picture 4), Sargent's 'Carnation, Lily, Lily, Rose' (Picture 30), Constable's 'Cloud Studies' (Pictures 16 and 17) and Ayres's 'Chanticlear' (Picture 41).

Picture 26

Katsushika Hokusai (1760-1849): Wild Sea at Chōshi, from series: Oceans of Wisdom (c.1832-3).
Musée National des Arts Asiatiques, Guimet, Paris; 29.3 x 19cm; coloured wood engraving.

AT1 main focus

POS: (ii)   *respond to memory and imagination using a range of media*
     (iv)   *experiment with ideas suggested by different source materials and explain how they have used them to develop their work*
     (v)   *apply their knowledge and experience in different materials, tools and techniques, using them experimentally and expressively*
     (vi)   *experiment with different qualities of line and tone in making images*
     (ix)   *experiment with ways of representing shape, form and space*

Art topic work/cross curricular links

The activities suggested can form part of an art-focused topic on Aspects of Landscape; see page 22.

Background information

This **print** was produced in a series entitled *'One Thousand Pictures of the Ocean'* (*Chie no umi*) published in about 1833. In fact only ten designs were carried out in print and these focus on the theme of fishing in all weathers.

The Japanese artist Hokusai thought that his best work was done after his 70th birthday, so that would include this print! When he died he had produced no less than 3,500 designs for prints and 250 illustrated books. This prolific career had begun when he was about 19 and had trained as a designer of prints with one of the leading graphic artists in his native Edo (present day Tokyo). He began his working life as an assistant in a book shop then trained as a cutter of wood blocks, but when he moved onto designing prints he did not cut his own blocks. Apparently there was clear demarcation of craftsmen involved at each stage of print publishing.

The publishing of illustrated books began to flourish in Japan in the 17th century but it was not until the end of that century that single prints were produced as works in their own right. The art of these wood block prints was known as *ukiyo-e*. There were two main themes for these: well known actors and fashionable courtesans, both of which continued into the next century. Hokusai's tutor designed prints of actors for example. Hokusai began in this vein but soon turned to other themes especially those of **landscapes, seascapes** and related activities based on the environs of Edo. Many of his patrons came from Edo's wealthy merchants who commissioned designs from Hokusai to be included in albums of their poetry.

Hokusai's prints were valued in his own lifetime but it was not until the 19th century that they reached a wider audience outside Japan. (Japan had remained a closed country barring all contact with other countries for almost 200 years before the Treaty of Friendship was issued in 1858.) Many prints initially arrived in the West as packaging for ceramics and other imports. They soon became objects of interest in their own right. Western European artists were encouraged by the example of Hokusai's work, amongst others, to adapt different **perspectives** and to break with established conventions in the **compositions** of their own paintings. Artists such as Manet, Degas and van Gogh paid tribute to the influence of Japanese prints in their work. The enthusiasm for oriental art in Western Europe in the mid-19th century also encouraged contemporary fashion in clothing and decoration to take on an oriental flavour.

Hokusai signed the print of 'A Wild Sea at Chōshi' at the bottom left and included the title at the top right. The achievement of such a beautifully balanced composition in which the two boats move precariously in the rising waves seems all the more remarkable given the design and printing process involved. Not only did each line of the artist's design have to be cut out of a wood block so that it stood out in **relief**, but also every colour required a separate wood block. Each colour was printed in turn, demanding considerable skill on the part of the printer to ensure that each part of the design was accurately aligned. Misalignment would result in fuzzy images and unclear colours.

Discussion

1.   Talk about the two fishing boats struggling in a wild sea. Ask the children how the artist has made the sea look wild. How has he suggested sea spray and lashing waves? Discuss which one of the people (there are six) in the near boat you would rather be and why. The person standing up is probably holding on to the net. Who seems to be doing this in the far boat? Do the children think the boats are moving in the same direction? Why/why not? How has the artist made you feel close to the water when you look at the picture? Can you see any land? (Remember that it would be very dangerous for the boats if they were too close to land.)

2.   Talk about the composition of the picture. Ask about the direction of the waves. Note how the movement is on the diagonal from top right to bottom left, so that the main boat is about to sweep out of the frame. This is a classic **open composition** which implies a continuation beyond the frame and therefore suggests the massive scale of the ocean beyond the area enclosed by the picture.

3.   Ask the children how many colours have been used in this picture. (They should be able to find six, not counting the white paper.)

4. Explain that this is a print not a painting and was printed from carved wood blocks, one for each colour (except white). Do you think this would be easy or difficult to do? What would require the most care? Although a lot of work is involved in print making ask the children if they think prints are cheaper than paintings. (Consider the number of copies it is possible to produce.)

5. The artist included the title of the print at the top right. It is rather difficult to see but ask the children to find where he put his own name. If you include writing on a print what do you have to remember? (A clue: the print is going to be a reverse image of the printing block.)

Practical activities

1. Create a work in which there is a similar sense of sweeping movement. This might be birds in flight (or the Red Arrows), fish shoaling, rain beating down, etc. Find back-up material by looking out for images that suggest movement and speed, such as blurred photographs of racing cars or runners at full stretch.

2. Make a collection of pictures of waves (from calendars, colour supplements, holiday brochures etc.) and compare them with Hokusai's print. Then paint your own picture of a wave, or make a pencil line drawing of waves at sea. Try to convey the swell and spray of a curling wave. Vary the thickness and length of lines to describe it. Do you think it would be easy to turn your drawing into a print?

Cross refer to watery pictures: Morisot's 'Summer's Day' (Picture 25), Lorraine's 'Embarkation of Saint Ursula' (Picture 24) and Bruegel's 'Fall of Icarus' (Picture 3).

Cross refer to pictures which convey movement: Hora (Picture 6), Constable's 'Cloud Studies' (Pictures 16 and 17), Rousseau's 'Tiger' (Picture 5) in *Approaches to Art, Key Stage One*.

Refer to *Approaches to Art, Key Stage One*, pages 74 and 75 for more detailed guidance on print making.

Picture 27

Achaemenian (Persian), (c.600-300 B.C.): Gold attachments from the Oxus Treasure (plaque, lion-gryphon disc and figurine), (c.600-300 B.C.). British Museum, London; approx. 2-5cm each in height, width and circumference; gold.

AT1 main focus

POS: (ii) *respond to memory and imagination using a range of media*
      (v) *apply their knowledge and experience of different materials, tools and techniques, using them experimentally and expressively*
      (viii) *experiment with pattern and texture in designing and making images and artefacts*

Art topic work/cross curricular links

The activities suggested can form part of art-focused topics on Working in Three Dimensions and Art for a Purpose; see pages 26 and 27.
The picture can also be used for work in History focusing on artefacts; see page 29.

Background information

The Oxus Treasure is so called because it was reputedly found scattered around in the sands of the River Oxus in Persia (now Iran). The treasure consists of 170 items, mostly made of gold or silver and dating from the 6th to the 3rd centuries B.C. The miscellaneous nature of the hoard is mysterious and no one knows who put it together or why. The treasure was found in 1877 and three years later it was nearly lost again when it was stolen by bandits from the merchants who were carrying it from Kabul to Peshawar. The merchants' servant raised the alarm however, in the camp of a British Captain Burton who came to the rescue. He found the bandits quarrelling over the hoard in a cave, and negotiated with them. As a result most of the hoard was saved, and after changing hands a few more times (legally this time) much of it ended up in the British Museum.

Whatever the origins of the treasure, it is an important collection because it shows many different styles of art and manufacturing techniques used in Persian society between the 6th and 3rd centuries B.C. It also indicates the great wealth of the society which was reflected in the dress and adornments worn by the king and nobility.

1.   Ask the children what they think these little thin gold **reliefs** were for. They were probably used for the embellishment of costumes and uniforms and on bridles and harnesses. Talk about any embellishments or decorations the children may be wearing today, things like badges, rings, ear-rings etc. Discuss situations in which those things have a specific meaning such as in Cubs or Brownie packs.

2.   **Miniaturisation** is of interest here. Talk to the children about the kinds of small (tiny) things they find attractive and why it is that they do so. What is it about small things, tiny toy people, doll's house furniture etc. that makes them exciting? Is it because they allow us to encompass reality at a glance, to take in a part of the world as a whole and intelligible experience?

Here, there is detail, but the scale of the objects and the technique allow only a kind of diagrammatic approach to detail, so that there is a satisfying chunkiness about the imagery.

3.   These bits and pieces are very old. Talk about B.C. and A.D. Work out how old they are. How is it that things like this survive from so long ago? Talk about things getting lost, natural and personal disasters. How would things like this end up in the sand at the bottom and at the sides of a river? While on this theme you could also talk about how people used to be buried with all sorts of valuables and how masses of the things we have got from the past actually come from tombs. Talk about tomb robbers and how, when people dig us up in thousands of years, they will be disappointed.

1.   Make your own versions of these objects.

i)   Take some aluminium foil. (Note that foil has a shiny side and a matt side.) Fold it in half and in half again, so that there are four sheets of it with the matt side facing up.

ii)   Draw your figure or design onto the foil using a Biro. Because there are four sheets you will be able to make quite an impression on the foil without tearing it.

iii)   When you have finished your image, take a pair of scissors and cut round the shape. Then gently peel off the top layer and look at it from the shiny side. It will look fabulous.

These are special tiny objects, almost like secrets. You could stick yours in a scrapbook, or you could make some ear-rings or a badge with them. For the latter, use a Sticky Fixer on the back. As a group project, you could decorate a complete figure with many of them. Draw a large Persian soldier on horseback, for instance, and decorate his uniform and trappings with them.

2.   Make a whole hoard of treasure out of gold and silver foil – include coins, attachments, swords, daggers, goblets, crowns, etc. Decorate the objects using **indentation techniques** similar to the Oxus treasures illustrated. Stick on jewels – glass jewels are quite cheap, old jewellery from junk shops, or boiled sweets. Half bury your treasure in a pile of sand. Draw or paint the hoard in the sand.

3.   Illustrate the story of the finding of the Oxus Treasure – episode by episode. Do this as a strip cartoon.

Picture 28

William Morris (1834-96): Acanthus and Vine tapestry (c.1879).
Kelmscott Manor, Gloucestershire; 188 x 244cm; tapestry.

AT1 main focus

POS: **(v)** *apply their knowledge and experience of different materials, tools and techniques, using them experimentally and expressively*
(viii) *experiment with pattern and texture in designing and making images and artefacts*
(ix) *experiment with ways of representing shape, form and space*

Art topic work/cross curricular links

The activities suggested can form part of an art-focused topic on Art for a Purpose; see page 27.

Background information

William Morris was an English artist, craftsman, designer, poet and social reformer. From his youth he was very interested in the Middle Ages and believed that the period exemplified a fusion of art with life. He was not just interested in medieval works of art but also in the society and craft methods which had brought them into existence. In 1861, he set up a firm (with friends) called Morris, Marshall, Faulkner & Co., 'Fine Art Workmen in Painting, Carving, Furniture and Metals'. The firm was established partly as a reaction against the mass production methods rife at the time. Later in his life Morris also became interested in social reform and he is considered to be one of the founding fathers of the British socialist movement. He was a man of extraordinary energy and when he died, at the age of 62, his doctor said the cause of death was due to his 'simply being William Morris and having done more work than most ten men'. It was partly due to him that the English Arts and Crafts Movement evolved.

Today Morris is particularly well known for his wallpaper and fabric designs, many of which are still in production.

In 1877 Morris had an 18th-century house on the banks of the river Thames at Hammersmith. It was called Kelmscott House (not to be confused with Kelmscott Manor in Gloucestershire where he also lived). At Kelmscott house Morris founded his first tapestry works and printing press.

109

The Acanthus and Vine tapestry is the first Morris ever produced. In its design, he was reacting against the type of tapestry that imitates painting. He felt that the tapestry technique did not lend itself to the creation of apparently three-dimensional images. He believed that the patterns produced in the Middle Ages were much more appropriate. So he looked at the work of medieval Flemish weavers, and created a **bilaterally symmetrical** pattern of stylised plant and bird forms. The plants are recognisably vines and less recognisably acanthus. Not surprisingly the tapestry acquired the nickname 'Cabbage and Vine'! The foliage is enlivened by birds of assorted sizes. The basic colours are blue and green.

To make the tapestry, Morris set up a loom in his bedroom and worked on it for 516 hours in 1879. It was the type of loom in which the back of the tapestry faces the weaver while the front is seen reflected in a mirror.

Morris's interest in the methods and techniques of the past led him to experiment with the production of **dyes** from vegetables and other natural sources. One of the consequences of the Industrial Revolution was the development of chemical dyes and **pigments** during the 19th century. Many of these were much more permanent (i.e. they tended not to fade) than their more naturally produced counterparts. Morris preferred the gentler more subtle colours of the natural dyes.

The firm went on to produce many notable tapestries all with a strongly medieval appearance.

Discussion

If you have *Approaches to Art, Key Stage One* you may find it useful to refer to Picture 20, which shows a detail from a late medieval/ **Renaissance** tapestry. This is the kind of work Morris would have been familiar with.

1. Ask the children what they think tapestries are. Explain that they are thick woven fabrics in which patterns or pictures are made in the **weft** stitches (which go across the **warp**). They were originally made to hang on walls, partly for decorative reasons, and partly to insulate the rooms. Because tapestries were expensive to make they were usually only found in the homes of the wealthy. Nowadays we value tapestries mainly for their decorative qualities.

2. Encourage the children to examine the picture closely. Can they see the threads? Can they describe the colours? Ask them if they think the colours were always like this? Talk about the possibility of fading. Point out the different sorts of plants, and let the children trace the plant forms with their fingers to find out how complicated they are. Ask which colours have been used most.

3. Ask what the children think about the way the pattern has been organised. Talk about the symmetry. This symmetry is bilateral, i.e. it is symmetrical from side to side, but the top half does not mirror the design on the bottom half. Ask the children if each side is exactly the same. Look for the differences, e.g. one main bird has its tail concealed by the acanthus leaves. Talk about how these differences came about – how within a sketch outline, the weaver is free to interpret in particular areas. Talk about colouring books and how everyone fills in the same outline image in a quite different and personal way.

1. Bilateral symmetry

Fold a piece of paper in half once, and unfold again. Put a small blob of colour on or near the fold, and then fold the paper along the existing fold firmly. Press down so that the spot of colour is squashed against both sides of the paper. When you open it up you should have a blot which is bilaterally symmetrical. Allow the blots to dry and then convert them into animals or plants, using pens or paints. Butterfly shapes often work well. However you do this, make sure the symmetry is maintained.

It is possible and effective to do this with more than one colour. You may find it useful to have a few 'goes' before doing the final version. It is a good idea to use cheap paper, at least initially. Scrap paper that is being discarded would be perfectly adequate.

For the final version you will find that the colour is easiest to control if you use paper which is rather porous – without too much surface gloss.

2. Natural Dyes

William Morris revived a number of traditional methods of making dyes from natural materials. In recent years there has been another revival of interest in this, and if you wish to explore it further the following three publications may prove useful: *A Dyer's Manual* by Jill Goodwin, (Published by Pelham, Steven Green Press, 1982/90); *Natural Dyes for Spinners and Weavers* by Hetty Wickens (Published by B. T. Batsford, 1983/90); *Natural Dyes: Fast or Fugitive* by Gill Dalby, (Ashill publications, Ashill Colour Studio, Jenny Dean, Boundary Cottage, 172 Clifton Road, Shefford, Beds. SG17 5AH).

Making natural dyes

There are numerous natural plant and animal substances which can provide dye colours – onion skins and cochineal beetles are among the best known.

To make a successful natural dye, which has depth of colour and some colour fastness, a **mordant** must be used in most cases. The mordant binds the dyestuff chemically to the material being dyed (e.g. wool). There are various mordants which can be used but we suggest Alum (with Cream of Tartar) which can be bought from a chemist.

Here are two recipes for dyeing wool using easily obtainable materials. Onion skins produce a yellow dye, and nettles produce a green one. Make sure the wool you intend to dye is not greasy and is wet before you add it to your dye pan. The amount of water you have in your dye pan does not really matter – there should be enough to cover the wool and for it to be moved around. Always wear rubber gloves.

The percentages given are proportional to the weight of material being dyed. So, for example, if 1kg of wool is being dyed you need 330g of dry onion skins and so on.

Yellow Dye.
Dyestuff – Dry onion skins 30%
Mordant – Alum 8% and Cream of Tartar 7%

(i)   First mordant the wool:
Dissolve the Alum and the Cream of Tartar in a little water. Put the mixture in a pan, add the damp wool and cover with water. Slowly bring to the boil over a period of about an hour and then simmer for about 45 minutes. Allow to cool. Rinse the wool and either use immediately or store damp in polythene for a few days until needed.

(ii)   Then boil the onion skins in a little water for 30 minutes. Cool and remove the skins. Add the pre-mordanted wool and more water if necessary. Bring to the boil over 45 minutes and then simmer for another 45 minutes. Leave the wool in the dye until cool, then remove it and wash it in warm, slightly soapy water. Rinse out the soap.

The same method can be used with nettles. Use the whole nettle – but not the root.

Green Dye.
Dyestuff – Nettles 200%
Mordant – Alum 8% and Cream of Tartar 7%

Cross refer to other types of Medieval art which inspired William Morris: silver-gilt casket (Picture 1), *Luttrell Psalter* (Picture 39) and bronze aquamanile (Picture 10).

Eugène Delacroix (1798-1863): Interior of a Moroccan House (1832).
Private collection; 15.8 x 21.3cm; watercolour and pencil on paper.

AT1 main focus

POS: **(i)**   *select and record images and ideas from first-hand observation*
(iii) *use a sketch-book to record observations and ideas*
(viii) *experiment with pattern and texture in designing and making images and artefacts*

Art topic work/cross curricular links

The activities suggested can form part of an art-focused topic on Observing and Responding; see page 23.

Background information

The 19th-century French artist, Delacroix, visited Morocco and Spain between January and June in 1832 and recorded his impressions of the countries in several sketch-books. He was fascinated by people's appearances (especially their clothes) and activities; by places – general views and individual buildings; by architectural details – exteriors and interiors and by the dazzling combination of rich colours and brilliant sunlight so much in evidence.

This interior is probably a room in the palace of Meknes where Delacroix stayed as a member of Count Mornay's entourage. Count Charles de Mornay had been sent by the new French king Louis-Philippe on a diplomatic mission to the Sultan of Morocco. Delacroix had himself received the Legion of Honour from the king for his painting 'Liberty Leading the People' which had made a great impact when exhibited at the 1830 Salon, the official annual exhibition for artists in Paris. (His often unorthodox subjects and methods of painting did not always win official approval.)

The impact of Morocco influenced Delacroix for the rest of his career. The intensity of its colours and exotic character fuelled his imagination and found expression in many of his later paintings. The emotional range and energetic handling of these works identified him with the **Romantic movement** in the arts. This sketch provides a glimpse of the energy he brought to painting and his eye for detail.

Delacroix has conveyed the **proportions** of the sumptuous room and the furnishings in the alcove through a combination of pencil drawing and watercolour **washes**, allowing the white paper to play an effective part in the description. The bold areas of white, for example, the inner right wall of the alcove and the edge of the entrance arch to the alcove, suggest the brightness of sunlight illuminating these parts. He conveys the pattern of the coffered ceiling and tiled walls by picking out the main shapes and repeating them where appropriate, but he does not attempt to paint every single part of the pattern each time it is repeated. This balance is one of the most difficult to achieve in painting and involves skilful judgement. He exercises it again when painting the shutter inset into the wall on the right of the alcove – there is just enough detail to enliven this part of the wall.

The sketch is annotated with Delacroix's notes on the actual colours and materials of the alcove, these include: *'porcel'* probably an abbreviation for 'porcelaine' referring to the tiled walls and *'velours pique amarente fonce'*, describing the deep pink stitched velvet of the divan cover.

Discussion

1. Ask the children to look closely at the sketch. What kind of room do they think it is? What sort of place might it be in? What suggests that it might be hot outside the room and cool inside? Is it something to do with the colours and light? What do they think the walls are covered with and what materials are the furnishings made of? Does it look comfortable? Would they like a window seat or divan like this? Why? What sort of person do they think would have a room like this?

2. You can generally find most of an artist's best ideas in his or her sketch-books. Ask the children what they think Delacroix was excited about when he made this study. Clearly the sumptuousness of the decoration was one appealing aspect, with the rich colourful tiles and fabrics, and the quality of both openness and intimacy about the architectural space.

3. Talk about whether it is possible to tell a sketch from a finished painting. What clues are given here that this is a sketch? Look at the way it has been drawn first and then painted. Can the children see any notes the artist made about the colours and materials of the room? Why do they think he made notes on the sketch?

Practical activities

1. Using coloured chalks or pastels make a sketch of a corner of the classroom or a room at home. Suggest the furnishings, curtains, wall colours etc., without putting in all the detail.

2. Make a sketch of part of a room and include a window. Concentrate on capturing the effect of light coming through the window and the shadows created, rather than the view through the window.

3. Make a collection of materials and objects which remind you of a hot place. Set up a **still life** (i.e. select a few of the objects and arrange them against a suitable background), and using pencil and paint make a sketch of it. Try to capture the main areas of light and shadow and suggest the shapes and patterns of the things in the group. Alternatively make a still life around a cool theme and sketch this.

4. Keep a notebook-cum-sketch-book in which you can make a note of things that have happened, which you may want to recall, and jot down ideas as they occur to you. This may be in written form, or it can be drawings or little painted studies of things you have seen or thought. When you see something that looks interesting but which you may not have time to record as completely as you want, try to put down enough information in the form of simple sketches and written notes so that you can recall it later. At other times you will have more time to make studies like the one from Delacroix's sketch-book. Sometimes ideas come when you are least expecting them and so it is important that your notebook should be small enough to carry around with you.

Cross refer to patterns and textures in: Vuillard's 'Woman in Blue' (Picture 2), Morris's tapestry (Picture 28) and the Indian Miniature (Picture 9).

Picture 30

John Singer Sargent (1856-1925): Carnation, Lily, Lily, Rose (1885-6).
Tate Gallery, London; 174 x 153.7cm; oil on canvas.

AT1 main focus

POS: **(ii)** *respond to memory and imagination using a range of media*
(vii) *apply the principles of colour mixing in making various kinds of images*

Art topic work/cross curricular links

The activities suggested can form part of art-focused topics on Observing and
Responding and Images of Self and Family; see pages 23 and 20.

Background information

John Singer Sargent was an American who travelled widely in Europe,
living for a while in Paris and then in London. He is particularly well
known for his **portraits**. He painted this picture while staying with
friends in the Cotswolds in the summer of 1885. He was recuperating
from a head injury. It was partly inspired by a garden he had seen one
evening on the Thames, which had beds of lilies and was hung with
Chinese lanterns.

It took Sargent more than a year to complete the picture, partly because
it was painted outside and he only worked on it for those few minutes
each evening when there was the right sort of mauvish light. The girls
(Dorothy on the left, and Polly) were the daughters of his friend, the
illustrator, Frederick Barnard.

Sargent wrote about the painting in a letter to his sister: 'Fearful
difficult subject. Impossible brilliant colours of flowers, and lamps and
brightest green lawn **background**. Paints are not bright enough, and
then the effect only lasts ten minutes'.

The title comes from a song popular at the time, 'The Wreath' by Joseph
Mazzinghi. The picture was exhibited at the Royal Academy Exhibition
of 1887 and was very well received.

1.   Ask the children what is in this picture. What are the girls doing? What time of day is it? What time of year is it? Is the garden these girls are in neat and tidy or rather wild? Identify the carnations (yellow), the lilies (white) and the roses (pink). What are the lanterns made of? (Paper.) How are they illuminated? (By candles.) Are the lanterns the brightest things in the picture?

2.   Talk about how the painting depends for its quiet, intimate mood, on the moment when twilight and artificial light combine to create a magical atmosphere in which time seems momentarily suspended and everything is poised and expectant. Introduce words such as 'twilight' and 'gloaming'. Discuss such moments with the children and talk about whether they might have had similar experiences of these kinds of lighting effects – visiting illuminations at a seaside resort perhaps, Guy Fawkes night, or even driving at twilight with their family.

3.   The light effects Sargent has achieved in this picture are extremely hard to do and it would be unreasonable to expect children to emulate these exactly, but it is well worth letting them have a go! There is a lot of scope to talk about, and work on, light and shade and light and colour, using this picture as a starting point.

It is worth noting that the lanterns, while illuminated, do not cast light on the things near them – there is too much background light for that. One of the reasons why the lanterns appear to glow, is the way the artist has contrasted their colour with the background colour. Look, for example, at Polly on the right. Where her lantern is against her white dress it almost disappears. The bright yellow/orange/pink of the lanterns stands out from the dark greeny/blue of the background. The colours Sargent has used are called **complementary colours** – the purples complement the yellows. They set each other off well and it is this that makes the lanterns appear to glow.

Practical activities

1.   Make paintings or pastel drawings on a dark **ground** (deep blue sugar paper for example) in which the black **silhouettes** of buildings, people or trees, for instance, are contrasted with moments of bright or subdued illumination. Perhaps draw people with torches or sparklers, cars with their headlights blazing or simply a row of street lights in the neighbourhood.

2.   Make colour wheels in order to understand the terms **primary colours**, **secondary colours** and complementary colours.

The primary colours are red, yellow and blue. They cannot be made by mixing other colours together. Secondary colours are made by mixing two primary colours together: red + yellow = *orange*; yellow + blue = *green*; blue + red = *purple*.

To make a simple colour wheel use the template on page 157. The sketch on the next page shows where to paint in the colours. Use very pure primary colours. (Teachers should try this out first and see which of the primary colours available produce the best and most vibrant secondary colours. Impure primaries produce dirty looking secondaries.)

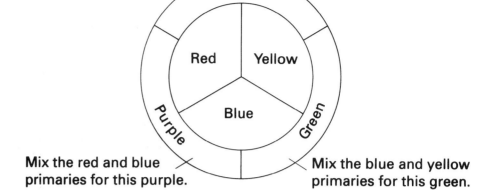

Mix the red and yellow primaries for this orange.

Mix the red and blue primaries for this purple.

Mix the blue and yellow primaries for this green.

Complementary colours are the ones which are opposites – so green (made by mixing yellow and blue) is complementary to red, etc. Used in conjunction with each other, complementary colours can produce very striking effects.

3. Experiment with colour contrasts.

i) Draw a lantern on a *white* piece of paper. There is no need to copy Sargent's Chinese ones. Invent your own but think carefully about size. If you are going to make a group picture out of these they will look best if they are roughly in scale with each other. To get good colour effects, make sure that they are large enough – approximately 10 to 20cm high.

ii) Paint the lantern as if it is illuminated. Discuss the colours Sargent used. To make the colours bright it is important that they are clean – not contaminated with other colours. Use pure white, yellows and oranges. Use clean brushes and have clean water.

iii) Allow the lanterns to dry and then cut them out.

iv) Using different coloured papers, put the painted lanterns against different coloured backgrounds. Which colours make the lanterns seem brightest? (You will find that dark colours make the lanterns seem light, but dark complementary coloured backgrounds will make them appear to glow.)

If you are feeling ambitious, a group of you can paint or make a collage of a large garden (or playground) to put the class's lanterns in. Use background colours that contrast best with the lanterns.

NB There may be some temptation to use flourescent paper/paint/ felt-tips here. Indeed these will create something of the same effect – more easily. If you do decide to use this late 20th-century device, let the children know that you are all *cheating* and that Sargent had no such materials to hand when he painted his picture!

Cross refer to Friedrich's use of darkness and light in Picture 23, and in Bening's illumination from *Da Costa Book of Hours* (Picture 15) in *Approaches to Art, Key Stage One*.

Bill Woodrow (1948-): Twin Tub With Guitar (1981).
Tate Gallery, London; 88.9 x 76.2 x 66cm; washing machine.

AT1 main focus

POS: **(iv)** *experiment with ideas suggested by different source materials and explain how they have used them to develop their work*
(v) *apply their knowledge and experience in different materials, tools and techniques, using them experimentally and expressively*
(ix) *experiment with ways of representing shape, form and space*
(x) *plan and make three-dimensional structures using various materials for a variety of purposes*

Art topic work/cross curricular links

The activities suggested can form part of art-focused topics on Images of Self and Family, Transformations, Observing and Responding and Working in Three Dimensions; see pages 20, 25, 23 and 26.

Background information

Much of Bill Woodrow's work explores the way in which objects such as old metal filing cabinets, or suitcases, for example, can take on a new significance by being transformed into other artefacts. He often uses clippers to cut into the metal sides of some defunct domestic machine in order to snip out and crudely fashion an entirely different kind of object. Sometimes the material he uses takes on a completely new character, as when a piece of vinyl from a sofa or suitcase becomes a pool of blood in its new art context. Some of his sculptures are simple transformations from one object into another. Others create complex **tableaux** from a number of different source objects.

One way of looking at Bill Woodrow's approach might be to compare it to that of the stone carver liberating an image from within the block of stone. Woodrow's tools are different but the perception is similar. His intuition sees the possibilities contained within the originating object and his imagination and creativity set about revealing it. The results of this process are often exciting and revealing. We bring to the sculptures a set of perceptions and meanings associated with the original object and with the object or image created. But when we see the juxtaposition of these in the same work, each alters the other, so that a whole new set of meanings is created. In some cases these invite speculation about the nature of society and about contemporary culture. In others, the meaning seems to centre on the more interior, psychological aspects of our nature.

Discussion

1. Explain that what we are looking at is a photograph of a twin tub washing machine which has had a guitar shape cut from its side. It is standing on a wooden floor against a buff coloured backdrop. The washing machine is a real one – if rather old fashioned in type. Ask the children if any of them have a washing machine like this one at home, or whether they know anyone who has one. What is a twin tub? Discuss the machine – one section washes, one spin dries and the openings are on top. Where are the controls? How can you tell this is an old machine? What sort of washing machines are more popular nowadays? What happens to old machines when they are worn out?

2. Talk about recycling. This machine has been recycled by the artist. When Bill Woodrow looked at the colour of this twin tub, he was reminded of the blonde colour of a guitar he had wanted when he was younger, so he constructed one for himself. This story demonstrates how ideas for art very often arise from quite personal or private memories and aspirations. It is important for children to recognise these kinds of inputs. Talk to the children about the way the idea for this sculpture arose and discuss with them the way ideas can be suggested simply by seeing something. Find some simple and/or unusual objects and discuss the kinds of things that they suggest.

3. Encourage the children to look carefully at how this work was done. What sort of tool would you need to cut metal in this way? The artist has not just cut a guitar shape out of the side of the machine, he has done other things too . . . what? Is it possible to work out how each cut out piece has been used and where it has been put? If you tried to push the guitar back into the machine, what would happen?

4. Where might one put a work of art like this? Would the children want it in their homes? In a church? In a palace? Think up a suitable place for it.

Practical activities

1. One of the interesting things about this area of Bill Woodrow's work, is that he has to have a clear idea in advance about where he is going to make his cuts, in order to fabricate his sculpture. This notion of creating a three-dimensional object from shapes cut out of a (largely) flat panel is a particularly interesting way of working for children at this stage. They can begin by making paper or thin card sculptures, designing and making simple box-shaped images like a car or a television, drawing in the details before cutting, folding and gluing them together. Then they might try to do some Bill Woodrow-like transformations, perhaps using cereal boxes as a starting point. From here the ingenuity of the teacher and the children will no doubt lead to all kinds of extraordinary recreations.

2.   Look at the kinds of transformations we undergo ourselves. Becoming an angel in a nativity play, for instance, or dressing up for Hallowe'en. Study the way actors and actresses have their faces modified in order to look different. Use face paints and devise and create new characters for your friends. Take photographs of them.

Cross refer to other images which involve transformations: Parmigianino's and Scrots's portraits (Pictures 14 and 15), Gilbert and George's 'Weather Window' (Picture 37) and Linares's 'Crab/Frog' (Picture 36).

Picture 32

Joan Miró (1893-1983): The Red Sun (1948).
Phillips Collection, Washington D.C.; 91.1 x 71.1cm; oil on canvas.

AT1 main focus

POS: **(ii)** *respond to memory and imagination using a range of media*
(vii) *apply the principles of colour mixing in making various kinds of images*
(ix) *experiment with ways of representing shape, form and space*

Art topic work/cross curricular links

The activities suggested form part of art-focused topics on Telling a Story and
Imagination and Invention; see pages 21 and 24.

Background information

Joan Miró is one of the major Spanish artists of the 20th century. He
was born in 1893 and became associated with the **Surrealist movement**
along with his contemporary Dali. His work has a look of **abstraction**,
though he has always been concerned to ground it in the everyday,
preferring to associate the forms on his canvas with those in nature.
From time to time Miró worked in the theatre and in later life produced
an extraordinary series of images in conjunction with the Las Clacas
theatre group. In this collaboration, the forms on his canvasses took on
a life of their own in the theatre, becoming a series of larger than life
characters with an enormous warmth and vitality.

Discussion

1. Ask the children what they can see in the picture. Some may say
the image in the black circle is a cat and that the creature immediately
below is a fish. Ask why. How much of an image do we need to be able
to recognise things? Some children might say that the image below
(with the red and black eye) is a bird because the thin black line
suggests wings. Discuss how it can make the picture more interesting if
you can see more things in it in this way.

2. The character on the right of the painting seems to have black boots and some kind of uniform or costume. Invite speculation on this character's role.

3. Discuss the colours. Talk about the use of blue and orange-red which are **complementary colours**. (Compare Miró's use of colour in this picture to Sargent's 'Carnation, Lily, Lily, Rose', Picture 30.) The use of the blue makes the red appear to glow more strongly then if another colour were used in the background. Talk about **transparency** and **opacity**. The blue paint is applied thinly as a **wash** on a white ground. The red is applied opaquely over the blue as are the yellow and white in the 'uniform' and the green surrounding the 'eye.

4. Can the children see anything in the picture which looks as though it is floating? Is there anything dream-like about the picture?

5. Discuss why the artist may have called it 'The Red Sun'. Do the children think this is a good name for it? Why? What title would they give it?

Cross refer to: Sassetta's 'Saint Francis' Dream' (Picture 38), *Luttrell Psalter* (Picture 39), Linares's 'Crab/Frog' (Picture 36) and Friedrich's 'Two Men Contemplating the Moon' (Picture 23).

Practical activities

1. Make similar paintings which explore the idea of transparency and opacity in paint. Apply washes in thin transparent colours onto white paper. (If you are using powder colour add some pva medium to the mix so that it doesn't dissolve again when you paint on top; otherwise use acrylics.) Allow these to dry then work on top in thick opaque mixtures. (You can produce opacity by adding white.)

2. Notice how the big black splodges in the middle of the work seem to suggest the body of a creature with the red face. Splash pictures: make some splash shapes by pouring some paint from a height (not too far!) on to paper. Let them dry and then see if they suggest anything to you. Work on top of them with paint, pen or pencil to turn them into recognisable forms such as animals, birds or people.

3. Think of an animal and talk about the visual qualities we associate with it. Draw just enough of a diagram that you think people will need to be able to recognise it. Talk about the places where you see pictorial signs of things, as on road signs, on ordinance survey maps etc.

4. Begin by drawing a pencil line on paper and continue by taking the pencil line 'for a walk' on the paper. Remember that you can cross backwards and forwards over the line but do not lift your pencil from the paper until you have finished. Are there any shapes you have made which remind you of a person or an animal? (Miró seems to have used this technique for the figure-like character at the bottom right.) Fill them in with different colours but limit yourself to four or five. Continue filling in some of the other shapes you have made but not all of them so that the patterns you make stand out clearly. See if you can make them appear to float.

5. Paint a picture which suggests something you might experience in a dream.

Picture 33

Giovanni Francesco Barbieri, known as Guercino (1591-1666): Aurora (1621-3).
Ceiling of principal room in Villa Ludovisi, Rome; fresco and tempera.

AT1 main focus

POS: (i)   *select and record images and ideas from first-hand observation*
(ii)   *respond to memory and imagination using a range of media*
(ix)   *experiment with ways representing shape, form and space*

Background information

Aurora, the Goddess of the dawn, drives her chariot across the sky, heralding a new day. In Ancient Greek mythology she is called Eos, the sister of Helios the sun-god. Here she strews flowers in her wake but is also crowned with a floral wreath by a flying putto (putti are winged babies often associated with Cupid). Cupid can be seen (upside down) taking aim with his bow at the bearded figure on the extreme left. This figure is usually identified as Tithonus, Aurora's husband. On the right are Aurora's female companions, traditionally identified as the Horae, goddesses of the seasons. (See the relief sculpture of a Hora on page 54.) The figures of the sleeping child and mother at the extreme right of the picture represent night, which is soon to be overtaken by the dawn.

This painting is on the ceiling of a room in a small villa in Rome. Another artist, called Agostino Tassi, was responsible for the painted architecture and foliage (based on the **landscape** around the villa). Tassi wanted to create the illusion of a room with no ceiling, open to the skies, so he continued the lines of the actual architecture of the room into his painted design. Guercino (which incidentally means 'with a squint') then painted the scene of Aurora. He continued the illusion of looking up into the open sky by painting the figures, chariot and horses as if they were seen from below. Such dramatic **foreshortening** required careful planning and skilful execution.

124

The villa, the Casino Ludovisi (which is included in the painting just below Aurora's chariot and clouds), was owned by Cardinal Ludovico Ludovisi, the nephew of the new Pope Gregory XV (formerly Cardinal Alessandro Ludovisi, Archbishop of Bologna). The Ludovisi family was from Bologna, where Guercino had trained as an artist and had already earned a reputation as a remarkable painter. His skills were acknowledged by the Carracci family, leading Bolognese painters. It was understandable that Guercino was summoned to Rome to work for the new Pope and members of his family but he returned to Bologna when Gregory XV died in 1623.

Tassi used the technique of **fresco** for his part of the design and Guercino used **tempera**. Fresco was the most common technique for **mural** painting. It literally means 'fresh' because the paint was applied on top of wet or fresh plaster. When the plaster dried the paint dried with it so that the painted design became an integral part of the wall. This was not the case with tempera. The **pigment** was mixed with the binding **medium** (here probably some form of animal glue and water rather than egg yolk), and was applied to dry plaster. It was more susceptible to flaking and so less durable than fresco, but Guercino's 'Aurora' has survived in excellent condition.

The dynamic, theatrical character of this painting is one of the hallmarks of **Baroque** art, which is the stylistic label often applied to art of the 17th century.

Discussion

1.   Encourage the children to look closely at this picture. Can they tell that it is painted on a ceiling? If so, how? What has the artist done to make you think there is no ceiling in this room? In fact part of the room looks like a ruin – can you see this part on the right?

2.   Do the children think the person in the chariot is an ordinary human being? What could she be? Who could she be? If she is Aurora, Goddess of the dawn, what time of day is this meant to be? Why do you think some of the clouds she is riding on, or near, are dark? In fact can you see a part of the picture which could be night time? What clues are there to help you? (Sleeping people, an owl, a bat.)

3.   Which of the colours the artist has used seem to fit the dawn best?

4.   Who do the children think the bearded man on the left is? Why do they think he's holding that piece of cloth in the air with the help of the winged baby? Can you find other winged babies in the picture? What are they doing? Can you find Cupid with his bow and arrow? Who is he aiming his arrow at? Why?

5.   Does it make a difference which way up one looks at the picture? What do you think the people who came in to the room would think when they looked up?

6.   Do the children think it would be easy or difficult to paint this picture? Why? What would the artist need? (Scaffolding and a good head for heights!) What sort of building could this room be in?

Practical activities

1.   Think of a subject which would make a good companion for this one (e.g. dusk, day, night, the sun) and paint a picture of it. What else would make a good companion – possibly a painting on the floor? Paint a picture for the floor of this room to go with 'Aurora' on the ceiling.

2.   Make some drawings of objects seen from below. Make some drawings of objects seen from above.

3.   Imagine the view that Aurora and her horses would get from up there. What do you think they would see down below? Why not paint a picture of their view.

4.   Imagine what it would feel like if you could float on clouds. Paint a picture of yourself and your friends having a party in the sky.

Cross refer to: Constable's 'Cloud Studies' (Pictures 16 and 17), Sassetta's 'Young Saint Francis' (Picture 38), Bruegel's 'Fall of Icarus' (Picture 3) and the sculpture of a Hora (Picture 6).

5.   Make some designs for your bedroom wall and ceiling and try to persuade your parents/guardian to let you paint them.

Picture 34

Paul Cézanne (1839-1906): Pommes Vertes (1873).
Louvre, Paris; 26 x 32cm; oil on canvas.

AT1 main focus

POS: **(i)** *select and record images and ideas from first-hand observation*
(vi) *experiment with different qualities of line and tone in making images*
(vii) *apply the principles of colour mixing in making various kinds of images*

Art topic work/cross curricular links

The activities suggested can form part of an art-focused topic on Observing and Responding; see page 23.

Background information

Paul Cézanne (1839-1906) was associated with the **Impressionist movement** early in his career. His work differs quite considerably from other Impressionist painters, such as Monet, in its adherence to some of the more formal and systematic methods of traditional painting. But Cézanne was unique in his use of colour and in the analytical way in which he looked for formal, almost **geometric** shapes within his **landscapes** in his attempt to come to terms with the forms of nature.

'Pommes Vertes' is a direct, fresh study which is full of vitality and acute observation. It is an excellent example of the kind of thing children can try out for themselves after looking at it closely and discussing the way it has been painted.

Discussion

1.   Get the children's first reactions to the painting (e.g. 'you could practically pick them up and eat them'), then ask about the lighting. Is it sombre, bright etc? What was the weather like if this picture was painted in natural light? If the classroom happens to be bathed in sunlight, get the children to look at the way light falls on various objects.

Compare the effect of the light on colour. Find an object like an apple and put it in direct sunlight and then in the shade so the children can see that the colours can become washed out where the strong light strikes the object, and that out of the direct light, the colours can be seen

127

more clearly but the **tones** are not so contrasted. In Cézanne's picture much of the joy of the study arises from it being bathed in bright light.

2.   The word 'juicy' could be used to describe the apples and the paint used to paint them. What makes them look juicy? Talk about other words which could describe the apples and the painting as a whole?

3.   The apples are described as green apples but the artist used more than one green to paint them. How many different greens can be seen? Why do the touches of red stand out so brightly on the left-hand apple? Talk about opposites or **complementary colours** here (refer to Picture 30 for more detail) and also about **warm** and **cool colours** (refer to Picture 4 for more detail). Where else has the artist used warm colours in the picture?

4.   Talk about the tones, from white to practically black, and about how you can manage to keep such contrasts when you are painting. For example, keeping white away from dark colours if you want them to stay deep in tone; keeping clean brushes and clean water (always use two jars each) for all tones especially light tones including white.

5.   Talk about the colours and how they too, have been kept fresh and un-muddy. Point out how this study has been made on a 'toned' ground (warm orange/brown) and this shows through in the gaps between brushstrokes, making a warm contrast to the greens of the apples.

6.   Ask the children whether the paint looks as though it has been put on thickly or thinly? Where does it look the thickest? How can they tell the artist has painted the picture on canvas? Can they see the **weave** especially where the paint is not so thick?

This type of painting where you can see the brushstrokes and the texture of paint is sometimes called a **painterly painting**. Compare it with other painterly pictures: Morisot's 'Summer's Day' (Picture 25), Ayres's 'Chanticlear' (Picture 41), Constable's 'Cloud Studies' (Pictures 16 and 17).

Compare this painting with other **still lives** (e.g. *Approaches to Art, Key Stage One*, Chardin and Picasso).

Practical activities

1.   After talking about all the above aspects of painting, make some still-life paintings from observation. Use simple shapes like these apples, and paint with thick brushes.

2.   The apples Cézanne used look rather like cooking apples. How many different colours of apples can you find? Make a display of apples and try out different colours of material or paper around them. See how their colours seem to change and choose which colour you think goes best.

3.   Make a collection of apples which have been painted, photographed or made, and discuss them.

4.   Compare the different roles apples play in stories and sayings – e.g. Snow White, Adam and Eve, 'An apple a day keeps the doctor away' and choose one to illustrate.

Picture 35

Scandinavian (mid 12th C.): Four Knights from the Lewis Chessmen (mid 12th C.).
British Museum, London; ht: approx. 8cm each; ivory.

AT1 main focus

POS: (v)   *apply their knowledge and experience of different materials, tools and techniques, using them experimentally and expressively*

(ix)   *experiment with ways of representing shape, form and space*

(x)   *plan and make three-dimensional structures using various materials and for a variety of purposes*

Art topic work/cross curricular links

The activities suggested can form part of art-focused topics on Working in Three Dimensions and Art for a Purpose; see pages 26 and 27.
The picture can also be used for work in History focusing on artefacts.

Background information

These figures are part of a collection of chessmen found on the Isle of Lewis in the Outer Hebrides in 1831. They were discovered in a small underground chamber on the south shore of the island and are thought to have belonged to an itinerant trader who hid them for safe-keeping.

The chessmen are carved out of walrus ivory and were probably made by a Scandinavian craftsman in the second half of the 12th century. Although the pieces are now uncoloured, when they were originally found there was evidence that some pieces had been stained dark red. During the 12th century, it was common to have either red and white, or red and green as gaming colours.

Altogether, 78 chess pieces were found, but not one complete set. Some figures, including these knights, are in the British Museum in London, others are in the National Museum of Antiquities of Scotland in Edinburgh.

Discussion

1. At Key Stage Two many children are learning how to play chess, joining chess clubs and playing in matches against other schools. It is appropriate at this stage for them to consider the notion that chess pieces, or indeed the objects and images used in other games, can be specially made as unique and individual art or craft objects and not just stamped out of plastic in their tens of thousands. One focus here, then, is on the idea that from a small block of ivory the maker has carefully crafted these individual characters which each have a special quality of their own. Talk about the differences between these characters (for example the horses, shields and facial details).

2. Look at the structure of these figures. Discuss how they need to be solid on their bases in order to sit squarely on the chessboard, and how they need to be of a similar size.

3. Look at photographs or other materials showing figures on horseback and talk about the kinds of simplification that had to be made in order for these knights to work as solid chess pieces.

4. Consider how these pieces would feel in the hand. Talk about the kind of things which feel good to hold. Talk about the way materials can be worn smooth by various forces. Discuss the idea that the game of chess is like a battle.

5. Talk about toy soldiers and discuss whether such things encourage a misunderstanding of the real nature of war.

6. These chess characters seem to have a lot in common with some of the larger-than-life, down-to-earth characters of early medieval drama. This is not likely to be a subject studied in English, though there may be opportunities to see some kind of community production. There are, of course, links here with things like Morris Dancing which may be more accessible. Also it may be worth exploring the simple narrative carvings seen in churches.

7. Consider the sources for ivory and the changing attitudes towards using it.

Practical activities

1. Making a chess set with the class. Model small-scale works in clay or carve into small cubes of plaster or lumps of chalk. Each child can be responsible for a particular figure, but it will be necessary to establish an overall plan and to decide on the scale of the characters. You might base your ideas on figures in an American Football team, for example, with their padded shoulders and helmets etc. or on the kinds of armour or uniforms worn in a period of history currently being studied. An all-female set of chess figures could be made. Alternatively, base your set on a school, including the Head, Deputy Head, teachers and children etc.

2. Extend the discussion about the 'feel' of the chessmen (mentioned above) by experimenting with the feel of different materials.

3. Focus on the individuality of each piece by dividing up modelling clay into balls and giving one ball to each member of the class. Squeeze each piece in the palm, release it carefully and allow it to dry. Each squeezed object will be unique to each child. Swap the objects and try out each other's, to see whether they work in the same way.

Picture 36

Felipe Linares (1936-), Leonardo Linares-Vargas (1963-), David Linares-Vargas (1963-): Crab/Frog (1989).
Location unknown; ht: approx. 60cm; paint and papier mâché.

AT1 main focus

POS: (ii) *respond to memory and imagination using a range of media*

(v) *apply their knowledge and experience of different materials, tools and techniques, using them experimentally and expressively*

(viii) *experiment with pattern and texture in designing and making images and artefacts*

(ix) *experiment with ways of representing shape, form and space*

(x) *plan and make three-dimensional structures using various materials and for a variety of purposes*

Art topic work/cross curricular links

The activities suggested can form part of art-focused topics on working in Three Dimensions and Imagination and Invention; see pages 26 and 24.

Background information

This figure is the work of the Linares family of Mexican sculptors, Felipe (b.1936), Leonardo and David (b.1963). They work in **papier mâché**, creating series of unique and strange mythological beasts and figures associated with the Mexican celebrations of All Souls Day (The Day of the Dead). Although this is predominantly a Catholic festival, it incorporates much from the rich diversity of Mexican culture, including elements from the Mayan and Aztec past. The images created by the Linares family subsume influences from many of the strands of Mexican culture and traditions, but they are also deeply personal images, many of them deriving from the visions of individual members of the family through the generations. They call their creatures the 'Alebrijes', an invented term that expresses the fictional world of the figures themselves.

Discussion

1. *Before* showing the children the picture discuss the difference between a hybrid and a chimera. A hybrid is the offspring of two different animals or plants which are sufficiently similar to be capable of breeding with each other – such as a mule or a liger for example. A chimera (apart from being a quite specific combination of, according to Homer, lion's head, goat's body and dragon's tail in Greek mythology) is a term applied to any animal or plant where part of one creature is

131

grafted onto another. In the case of plants, botanists actually do this. For example, you can take the root-stock of an apple tree and graft onto it sections of lots of different apple trees. In this way you can grow many different varieties of apple on one tree. This tree could be called a chimera. In the case of animals, all chimeras are fantasies.

Now show the children the picture. Would they call this a hybrid/a chimera/both or neither? The creature is called a crab/frog but which parts of it seem to belong to which and which belong to neither?

2.   Talk about the character of this beast. Is it frightening or funny or both? Would you feel differently about it if it were 12 metres high? Would you like one of these as a pet? Do you think it lives on land or in the water? How do you think it moves about – does it waddle, leap, swim, fly? What sort of noise do you think it makes? If it could talk, what do you think it would be saying? What do you think it likes to eat? Is it carnivorous or herbivorous? Think up a suitable name for it. What sort of home do you think it lives in – a nest, a hole, a tree, a cave, in seaweed or what? Does it lay eggs or have live young? Is this a baby or a grown up? Is it male or female?

3.   Find photographs of masks in mosaic from the Aztec civilisation (most Key Stage Two history Exploration and Encounters textbooks will have them), and look at the patterning and decoration on them.

Practical activities

1.   Create a home for this creature. (Use the template on page 158 for a cut-out of the animal.) Stick the creature onto a piece of paper and create an environment around it – perhaps outside, under the sea or in a cave. Work secretly so that you do not influence each other. Use paint or collage.

2.   Create a chimera by using separately recognisable elements (for example human head, giraffe's neck, bird's body, gorilla's arms, table legs, regular shoes, etc.) from a range of different sources. Do this in drawing, or using **photomontage**, cutting out things that might make good legs, arms etc. and sticking them down.

3.   Make a model of your own hybrid/chimera using chicken wire and plaster. (Recommended for top juniors only.)

First make the shape of your creature by bending and squeezing chicken wire into the shape you want. This can be difficult. Do not be too ambitious. (The teacher should try it out first to be aware of the pitfalls and beware of the scratchy edges.) Then there are two ways of proceeding – with either papier mâché or plaster of Paris:

1)   Plaster of Paris. When the wire is in the shape wanted, bind fine muslin tape (the sort used for bandages) round the wire, all over. This gives the plaster of Paris something to hang onto and makes it easier to work. Then either dip the model into a pot of liquid plaster or apply liquid plaster with a spatula. Allow the plaster to dry. Painting can start when the plaster is touch-dry.

2)   Papier mâché is easier to handle as squares of paper can be applied with paste one by one. You can build up and shape the creature with more freedom and make more alterations to your original wire model than you can with plaster. The model must be completely dry before paint is applied. This may take some days.

Cross refer to other imaginative creatures and settings: Miró's 'The Red Sun' (Picture 32), Friedrich's 'Two Men Contemplating the Moon' (Picture 23) and Blake's 'The Tyger' (Picture 22).

Picture 37

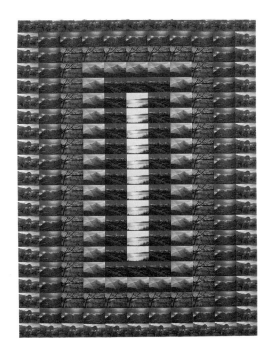

Gilbert and George: Weather Window (1989).
Private collection; 241 x 182cm; postcards.

AT1 main focus

POS: **(iv)** *experiment with ideas suggested by different source materials and explain how they have used them to develop their work*

(viii) *experiment with pattern and texture in designing and making images and artefacts*

Art topic work/cross curricular links

The activities suggested can form part of an art-focused topic on Transformations; see page 25.

Background information

Gilbert (b.1943) and George (b.1942) are artists who have worked together since studying sculpture at St Martin's School of Art in London in the late 1960s. They have always adopted a studied and formal approach to their life which they would consider as inseparable from their art. In public they always appear in almost identical, slightly archaic looking suits, giving them a mannequin-like appearance. They come across as polite, well-mannered and, to some extent, reserved. Their work has a similarly studied quality in the sense that it is clearly conceived and carried through. But it is also passionate in its commitment and in the power and clarity of its imagery.

Their large-scale pictures, which are photo-works incorporating both photographic images and diagrams in a **composite** of black-framed rectangles, are often brightly coloured in saturated **primary** and **secondary hues** which glow within the black forms and outlines of the images like stained glass. The imagery is often uncompromisingly frank and always clear. Their work explores universal themes of sex, life and death, nature and culture and the power of the imagination.

But it does so in a startling and entirely contemporary way. Gilbert and George are cool and acute observers of their time and they seem to achieve this detachment by being at the very centre of their own work. They have made many performance works in addition to appearing in most of their photo-works.

'Weather Window' comes from a series of 'postcard' pictures made in 1989. For each of the pictures, Gilbert and George selected a number of commercially available postcards and arranged them to form a composite image.

Discussion

1.   Begin by showing the image from a distance and asking the children what they think it is. The chances are that one may say it is a rug or carpet. Talk about the effect of the pattern from a distance. Does it look flat? Why does it seem to come forward or go back in places? Talk about the effects of light and dark tones and of the bright yellow vertical in the centre which seems to illuminate the whole image. Talk about the colours and ask the children to identify the kinds of colours used in the work e.g. red/blues, yellow/blues etc.

2.   The children can then look at the picture close-up and suggest what the image is made of. Look at the individual postcards close-up and talk about the seasons that are represented, the possible times of day, the weather, the type of countryside etc.

3.   Talk about pattern and repetition. Where can the children see examples of repeating units being used in decoration? For example, on local church floor tiles, mosaics, wallpaper, curtain material etc., and also in art such as Andy Warhol's Brillo boxes, Carl Andre's flat floor pieces etc. Pattern and repetition can also be seen on the shelves of supermarkets and DIY stores.

Practical activities

1.   Make the equivalent of your own postcard pieces. If you can't get hold of lots of postcards, find images from magazines, brochures, comics, holiday snaps, etc. and make lots of photocopies of them. Here, Gilbert and George have used the theme of 'Weather', but you can choose your own theme, for example music, family, or animals. Cut the photocopies to the same size so you can stick them down in your own patterns in a rectangular format.

2.   The play between 'close-up' and 'far-off' can be further explored in practical work in which the children collect piles of 'colours' from magazine cuttings. A 'red' might come from an advertisement for a car or from a landscape image. Make pictures by sticking down these colours in particular arrangements. You might make a big face, for instance, with red hair. When you look at it from a distance it just looks like a mass of red hair, but from close-to you can see that it is made up from images of cars, flowers, fabric etc.

Cross refer to other landscape pictures: Gainsborough's 'Mr and Mrs Andrews' (Picture 4), Morisot's 'Summer's Day' (Picture 25), Bruegel's 'Fall of Icarus' (Picture 3) and 'Baz Bahadur and Rupmati' (Picture 9).

Picture 38

Stefano De Giovanni, known as Sassetta (c.1392-1450): The Wish of the Young Saint Francis to become a Soldier (between 1437 and 1444).
National Gallery, London; 87 x 52.4cm; egg tempera on wood.

AT1 main focus

POS: **(ii)** *respond to memory and imagination using a range of media*
(viii) *experiment with pattern and texture in designing and making images and artefacts*
(ix) *experiment with ways of representing shape, form and space*

Art topic work/cross curricular links

The activities suggested can form part of art-focused topics on Images of Self and Family and Telling a Story; see pages 20 and 21.
The picture can also be used as a stimulus for creative writing; see page 32.

Background information

Stefano De Giovanni, known as Sassetta, was one of the leading artists in Siena, Tuscany in the 15th century. In 1437 he was commissioned to paint the large altarpiece from which this panel comes. The contract made between him and the friars of the Franciscan Church, San Francesco, in the small town of Borgo Sansepolcro, Tuscany, still exists. It states that Sassetta was to complete the altarpiece within four years, use the finest materials and his greatest skill. The altarpiece was finally delivered seven years later in 1444. (It is interesting that the friars looked to Siena rather than Florence for their altarpiece, since Florence in the 15th century was a major centre of developments in the arts identified with the **Renaissance**. This may suggest an element of conservatism in the friars' choice of artist.)

This painting is one of eight showing scenes from the life of Saint Francis. The scenes are thought to have been arranged on either side of a central image of Saint Francis on the back of the altarpiece. On the front were the Virgin Mary, Christ Child and Saints. Seven of the eight scenes are now in the National Gallery, London and one is in The Musée Conde, Chantilly.

135

This scene shows the first two episodes in the sequence, which is why Saint Francis appears twice: 1. Saint Francis giving his coat to a poor knight; 2. the dream of Saint Francis. Saint Francis came from a wealthy family and had thought he would become a soldier, but an angel appeared to him in a dream to explain that he was destined for a different course of action. He was to found an Order of Friars dedicated to preaching the gospels and living by the vows of poverty, chastity and obedience.

The episodes from Saint Francis's life (1181-1226) were based on the official biography written 1260-1263 by Bonaventura, Master General of the Franciscan Order. Further events and themes were expanded upon later in the 13th century, with writings such as *The Little Flowers of Saint Francis* mentioning his preaching to the birds and kindness to animals.

Like most holy figures in Christian art Saint Francis and the angel are shown with haloes representing a glory of light around their heads. Haloes of luminous circles can be seen around the sun or moon when light is refracted through mist.

Materials and Techniques
The **medium** Sassetta used for painting this panel was egg **tempera**: egg yolk was used with a little water to stick or bind powdered coloured **pigment** together to make paint.

The wooden panel, or **support,** had to be prepared before painting began. Once the panel was cut to shape and smoothed down it was sealed with glue size (made from animal skins) and then painted with layers of **gesso** (gypsum or calcium sulphate mixed with glue size). This hardened rather like plaster of Paris. Each layer of gesso was carefully smoothed down to provide an even foundation (**ground**) for painting on.

The next stage was **gilding** the panel. All the gold in the picture is real gold, i.e. **gold leaf**. All areas to be gilded were painted with a red coloured clay pigment called **bole** which helped enrich the appearance of the gold leaf applied on top of it. This can sometimes be seen where the gold leaf has worn away. Other metals were sometimes used and there are traces of **silver leaf** on Saint Francis's gown. If silver survives on paintings like this it has usually oxidised and turned black.

The pattern on the gold haloes of Saint Francis and the angel were made by **punching**, that is, using a metal punch to press a design into the gold. The pattern of stars on the bed, and the patterns on the bed clothes and Saint Francis's gown were done in **s'graffito**. In this technique the artist painted a colour such as red or blue on top of gold or silver leaf then scratched a pattern or motif out of the paint layer to reveal the gold or silver beneath.

Discussion

The painting is particularly useful in connection with storytelling through pictures, ideas of sequence and time, and use of the imagination.

1.   Point out that here there are two episodes from a story about Saint Francis. Consider how the artist has separated the two: one is outside, the other inside; Saint Francis appears twice, doing different things; one is day time, the other night time, or seems to be (Francis is asleep in his bed which is painted with stars).

136

2. Ask the children what they think is happening in each episode. Which episode does the floating castle seem to belong to and why? (It is more likely to be in a dream, and the angel points up to it.)

3. Why do the children think the artist painted the sky around the castle to look like daylight rather than night time? Would it have looked strange if he had painted it half and half?

4. Saint Francis and the poor knight are standing in the road in the **foreground**, of the picture, which leads to the walled town in the **background**. Which of the two would feel most uncomfortable on this stony road? What is Francis wearing on his feet and why? How much of his horse can be seen?

5. The artist had to fit everything into the shape of the panel he was given. How would the children have **composed** it?

6. Discuss whether you automatically follow the sequence of the story from left to right. If so, why? Are there other ways of reading it?

Practical activities

1. Discuss the fact that in the one picture, the same figure is shown at different times and that there is a castle floating in mid-air. Find parallels to this in contemporary work, comics, television and films etc. Then draw or paint a picture showing two or three different things that you might have done in one whole day; remember to include yourself as many times as necessary and follow as clear a sequence as possible. You can suggest time and space by the way you use the foreground and background.

2. Make a work which shows the inside and the outside of your house at the same time and also shows in picture form what the people in the house are thinking (or dreaming, as in the case of Saint Francis). Notice that the interior has an 'interior' exterior in the night sky in s'graffito above the bed.

3. Saint Francis's gown originally looked much brighter and richer than it does now. Design a splendid outfit for him or for someone else using the s'graffito technique to create pattern and texture: use wax crayons first then paint a dark colour over the crayoned design and scratch a pattern through the dark paint to reveal the colours beneath.

4. Compare the castle Saint Francis dreamed about with other pictures of castles and then make a picture of an imaginary castle you would like to explore.

Cross refer to: John Martin's 'The Bard' (Picture 8), Claude Lorraine's 'Seaport' (Picture 24), Boccaccio's *De Claris Mulieribus* (Picture 19).

Picture 39

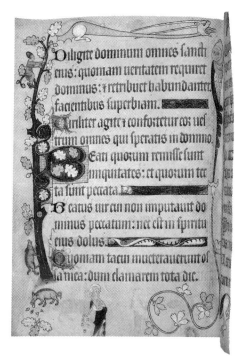

English (East-Anglian) (14th C.): The *Luttrell Psalter*: page showing swineherd feeding acorns to pigs (Ms 42130, ff 59v), (c.1340).
British Library, London; 36 x 24cm; illuminated manuscript.

AT1 main focus

POS: **(i)** *select and record images and ideas from first-hand observation*
(iv) *experiment with ideas suggested by different source materials and explain how they have used them to develop their work*
(vi) *experiment with different qualities of line and tone in making images*

Art topic work/cross curricular links

The activities suggested can form part of an art-focused topic on Transformations. The picture can also be used in connection with work on presentation (English AT3) see page 32.

Background information

This is a page from a book which was made in the early 14th century. A 'psalter' is a personal prayer book, and this one was made for Sir Geoffrey Luttrell who lived in Lincolnshire. We know this because of the **heraldry** on one of the pages. (Refer to pages 40 and 41 for more detail about heraldry.) The psalter contains psalms and canticles (hymns) in Latin, preceded by a calendar, and followed by a litany (a series of petitions for use in church services and processions, recited by the clergy and responded to by the congregation). It also contains collects (short prayers) and the Office of the Dead (funeral service) with music.

The book consists of 309 leaves of well prepared **vellum**, each measuring approximately 360 by 245mm. Over 200 of these pages have decorated margins which show a combination of biblical scenes, scenes of everyday life and pure fantasy.

The terms 'vellum' and '**parchment**' (skin) are interchangable. The word 'vellum' has the same origin as 'veal' – in other words 'calf' – so vellum is calf-skin. In fact it is usually impossible to tell what sort of skin has been used in old manuscripts and doubtless sheep, goat, deer and pig skins were also employed.

138

The preparation of vellum was a long and complicated process. The chosen skins were washed, the hair removed, dried and stretched. Good parchment is soft, thin, unblemished and folds easily. It is extraordinarily durable and can last for 1000 years or more in perfect condition. The side of the skin where the hair once was (the **grain** side) often echoes the colour of the hair and it tends to curl in on itself, the flesh side is usually lighter.

A book was not made up of single pages, but pairs of **leaves** (**bifolia**). Several such pairs were put together, folded down the middle, one inside another and then stitched along the fold. Each of these is called a **gathering** or **quire**. (The *Luttrell Psalter* has 26 quires of mostly 12 pairs of leaves.) The leaves were always arranged so that grain sides faced each other. When a book is open, the right-hand page is called the **recto**, the left **verso** (i.e. it is the reverse of the recto).

Lines were ruled on the pages for the scribe to write on. You can just make these out after the last word on the page in the Group Discussion Book. Notice there are two lines drawn to give the height of the body of the letters. The writing was, of course, done by hand, using a pen probably made from either a quill or a reed. The best quills came from the outer pinion wings of geese or swans. (Turkey quills are of the highest quality, but because these birds come from America they were unknown in Medieval Europe.)

Ink was made from either carbon (charcoal or lampblack) mixed with gum, or from a mixture of tannic acids (which were obtained from 'oak apples' or galls made by the gall wasp), with ferrous sulphate and gum. The recipes involved time and skill. Red ink was made from vermilion – a naturally occurring mineral which was also manufactured from an early date.

Discussion

1.   Talk about this being a handwritten and hand-drawn page from a book which was made for a very rich person over 600 years ago. All such books from this time are unique (explain this word if necessary). It is written in Latin and it contains prayers and other religious material.

2.   Point out how even the writing is and how the capital letters are made to stand out. Ask the children which one stands out the most. ('B' of 'Beati', which means blessed.) How are the Ss embellished? How are the margins of the page decorated?

3.   How many people can the children see? Which one is Holy? How can you tell? Do you think the person in the tree is a man or a woman? What is he or she doing? (The person is a swineherd, knocking acorns off the trees for the pigs.) How are the pigs different from modern breeds? What season is it? What can you see peeping out of the hole in the tree? (It is an owl.)

Does the lady at the bottom of the page seem to have anything to do with the swineherd? (She has a halo and seems to be carrying a rosary made out of teeth – we are not sure who she is – Saint Apollonia was tortured by having her teeth extracted but she is usually shown holding pincers!) What other creatures can you find on this page?

Practical activities

For older juniors:
1.   Make a quill pen. (A teacher may need to assist when a sharp knife is used.) No medieval instructions for making quill pens survive – probably every literate person knew how to do it.

i)   Use strong flight feathers and dry them well.

ii)   Trim away the thin end and most of the barbs, the outer skin and the pith inside the barrel, to leave a strong tube.

iii)   Think about what a fountain pen nib looks like and use a sharp knife to cut off the tip of the quill. Make a shallow scoop along the underside of the quill and cut a central slit in the nib.

iv)   Shape the nib on either side of the slit.

v)   If required, make a reservoir for the ink by attaching an s-shaped piece of metal under the scoop. (This can be cut-out from a ring-pull on a can.)

2.   Use this page as a starting point for discussing beautiful handwriting. (See also 'The Tyger' by Blake, Picture 22 and 'The Arnolfini Marriage' by van Eyck, Picture 13.) A book on **calligraphy** would be very helpful here. Your local library may be able to get one for you.

Discuss different styles of script, such as **Italic, Uncial** etc. If possible give the children some examples to copy. (The templates on pages 159 and 160 may be useful here.) Let them write their first name in the script of their choice. Give them lined paper, ideally with double lines to help them get the letters the same size as each other. They could use pens (quill or dip) with, for example, italic nibs. You can also get italic felt-pens these days.

3.   Having perfected a beautiful script make an illuminated page. Four short lines of text is enough. Use paper with wide margins all around and faintly drawn pencil double lines in the middle so they can be rubbed out later. Then choose the text. You could combine this with poetry, or work on 'sayings' or proverbs in English.

Write the text as beautifully as you can and embellish the capitals and some of the other letters. Then do some illustrations in the margins, which relate to the meaning of the text. The use of small and imaginative details can be very effective.

4.   Discuss the way the artist has filled in the gaps at the end of each verse, before the new verse begins and at the top, bottom and side, with strange beasts and figures. Allow your imaginations to run riot in the same way by decorating an existing page in an exercise book which only has writing on it. Make it into something sumptuous.

For younger juniors:
1.   Making a decorated page is quite difficult and we suggest that if you are going to attempt it with under nines, it would be helpful to provide a very faint version of the chosen text for the children to go over in bold. Freehand beautiful script really is very difficult to do, and young children will be discouraged by their inability to do it well. To give them a helping hand in this way will make them feel successful and encourage them to do it on their own later on.

Fra Filippo Lippi (c.1406-1469): Portrait of a Man and a Woman at a Casement (c.1440).
Metropolitan Museum of Art, New York; 64.1 x 41.9cm; tempera on wood.

AT1 main focus

POS: (i) *select and record images and ideas from first-hand observation*
(iv) *experiment with ideas suggested by different source materials and explain how they have used them to develop their work*
(viii) *experiment with pattern and texture in designing and making various kinds of images*
(ix) *experiment with ways of representing shape, form and space*

Art topic work/cross curricular links

The activities suggested can form part of an art-focused topic on Portrait (Images of Self and Family); see page 20.
The picture can also be used when focusing on using pictures as evidence in History, see page 28.

Background information

It seems ironical that the present title of the painting puts the man first, since the woman is the dominant figure. The identity of this woman and man are not known. Both are shown in **profile**, the favoured view for **portraits** in Italy at this time.

The **Renaissance** period (15th and early 16th centuries) was characterised by a revival of interest in the ideas and concerns of the classical past and particularly of the art and literature of Ancient Greece and Rome. According to the Ancient Roman writer Pliny in his book *Natural History*, the art of painting began 'with tracing an outline round a man's shadow'. This refers to the portrait in profile made by the daughter of a man called Butades. The daughter was in love with a young man who was to go abroad. She wanted to have an image of him which she could look at while he was away so she illuminated his face by lamplight and drew around the shadow of his profile cast against the wall. Butades took the profile portrait a stage further when he pressed clay into his daughter's outline drawing and made a relief of the young man's head. This anticipated the representation in profile of emperors on medals and coins (a tradition which continues up to the present, on stamps for example).

Since Ancient Roman coins, medals and relief sculptures were among the classical objects collected enthusiastically by wealthy Italians during the Renaissance, it is not surprising that they should commission portraits in profile too. It is still acknowledged that the most distinctive view of a person is their profile (think of the use made of this for criminal records today as well as for cameos and **silhouettes**).

The clothes and jewels of the woman indicate her wealth and rank. She is fashionably dressed, with her hair pulled right back from her face and covered by an elaborate head-dress. (Exposed foreheads were considered beautiful and sometimes women shaved their hair to emphasise the forehead.) This head-dress is similar in structure to that of Giovanna Cenami (see 'The Arnolfini Marriage', Picture 13), except the horns of this one are fixed further back rather than projecting out at the side. She is wearing two dresses: the under dress of dark material has full embroidered sleeves; the over dress, possibly of red velvet, is trimmed with fur. Letters picked out in pearls and gold thread around the edge of the over sleeve may be part of the woman's family motto and would help identify her. The man rests his hands on an embroidered cloth with a shield and lettering around the edge which could also identify him. The shield has been identified with that of the Scolari family, one of the wealthier Florentine families. It has also been suggested that the picture was commissioned to mark an engagement or marriage.

The artist who probably painted the picture was Fra Filippo Lippi, one of the leading artists in Florence towards the middle of the 15th century. He had been brought up in the Carmelite (reformed Benedictine) monastery in Florence where Masaccio's famous **frescoes** were painted on the walls of the Brancacci Chapel. Filippo Lippi may well have been inspired to pursue his interest in painting by Masaccio's example if not by Masaccio himself. Vasari, one of the earliest biographers of Italian artists, described Lippi's life in colourful detail including his amorous liaison with a nun, Lucrezia Buti, which resulted in a son, Filippino Lippi, who also became a painter!

 **Discussion**

1.   Ask the children what they think this situation is. Do they think the picture was painted simply to record the appearances of these people, or to mark or celebrate an event such as an engagement or wedding?

2.   Discuss whether the man and woman are looking at each other. If not, why not? The picture does seem to beg the question how two people so close to one another appear not to be noticing each other at all. Perhaps there is a serious relationship issue here?

3.   Talk about the physical space depicted in the painting. How much of each person can be seen? (This type of portrait is usually described as a **half-length portrait**.)

Is it a window or a picture on the wall behind the woman? What might the man be standing in or on (i.e. another room/a balcony/a ladder)?

4.	Ask the children to look carefully at the woman. How can one tell that she is wealthy? How many rings has she got? Does her head-dress look comfortable? Why? Would it have been easy to move around in the clothes she was wearing?

Talk about the statuesque aspect of the woman's pose. Her rich, fine clothes, jewels, head-dress and elegant hairstyle give her an air of authority and composure.

5.	Discuss the man's appearance, and look carefully at the cloth he is leaning on. (Compare this detail with the heraldry shown on the casket in Picture 1.) Ask the children what the letters around the edge of the cloth could be spelling out.

6.	Draw attention to the fact that both faces are shown from the side (i.e. in profile). Compare the two profiles by examining the angle of the foreheads, the shape of the noses, the size of the mouths, the shape of the chins etc.

7.	Ask the children what they think the **focus** of the painting appears to be. Certainly the woman's profile is the brightest and clearest part of the work.

Practical activities

1.	Work in pairs. First, one of you draw the head and shoulders of your partner in profile, paying particular attention to the shape of head, hairstyle, forehead, nose, lips, eyes and eyebrows, and then swap over. Everyone's drawings could be put on the wall to see if the class members can recognise each other from their profiles.

2.	After drawing your friend's profile, turn it into a more detailed picture. Decide what shape you want to make it and what else you are going to put in it (you could leave the background plain of course). Would you include any lettering or inscriptions? You could still work in pairs but would need to work out the best way of arranging both your profiles within a frame. You will have to decide what shape you would like the frame to be, for example square, rectangular, oval etc. Instead of painting a frame perhaps you could make a **collage** of one from metal foil or other coloured paper. In fact you could make the whole picture a collage. Choose materials carefully to suggest the colour and texture of your friend's features and clothes.

3.	Trace the outline of a profile you have drawn onto black or another deeply coloured paper and cut it out to make a silhouette. Then stick the silhouette onto contrasting paper. You could make a frieze of silhouettes to go around the classroom or one whole wall panel. You could vary the directions of the profiles and perhaps add some captions.

4.	Draw a friend's profile then add a superb head-dress of your own design. You might base this on a medieval knight, a native American Indian, a medieval woman or any other source, or you might make it up completely. You could make a series of cut-out head-dresses which could be superimposed on your profile, changing its identity completely from one to the other.

5. Use clay to make a **relief** version of your friend's profile. You can suggest the texture of your friend's hair and clothes by drawing into the clay with wooden or metal tools or building them up with more clay.

6. You could design a new coin or medal including a profile portrait.

7. See if you can work out how to draw your own profile – you may need to use mirrors or a lamp for this.

8. Make a collection of profile portraits/pictures from objects you can find at home and school (e.g. magazines, stamps, mugs, brooches, coins, medals). These may give you more ideas for your own profile pictures.

9. Consider ways of animating Lippi's picture, perhaps in the form of a model theatre with the two characters as cut-out paper puppets with movable arms. Could there be other characters waiting in the wings and what would happen if the scene behind them changed?

Cross refer to other representations of a woman and man: 'Baz Bahadur and Rupmati' (Picture 9), Jan van Eyck's 'The Arnolfini Marriage' (Picture 13), Gainsborough's 'Mr and Mrs Andrews' (Picture 4) and Moore's 'King and Queen' (Picture 7).

Cross refer to other profiles: Scrots's 'Edward VI' (Picture 15), Boccaccio's *De Claris Mulieribus* (Picture 19).

Picture 41

Gillian Ayres (1930-): Chanticlear (1988-9).
Property of the artist; 106 x 106cm; oil on canvas.

AT1 main focus

POS:
(ii) *respond to memory and imagination using a range of media*
(v) *apply their knowledge and experience of different materials, tools and techniques, using them experimentally and expressively*
(vii) *apply the principles of colour mixing in making various kinds of images*
(viii) *experiment with pattern and texture in designing and making various kinds of images*

Background information

Gillian Ayres decided that she was going to be a painter when she was 14, having visited 'Painting of the Month' exhibitions at the National Gallery during the Second World War. She enrolled at Camberwell School of Art in 1946 and has been involved with the practice and teaching of painting ever since. In 1982 she was made an Associate of the Royal Academy and awarded an O.B.E. in 1986. She lives and works in London and North Devon.

One of the most important influences on her work as an art student was a photograph. The photograph showed the American artist Jackson Pollock at work in his studio. Jackson Pollock had pioneered a form, or rather a process, of painting which had been called **action painting**. Working on a large scale on the floor of his studio, he dripped, flicked and poured paint onto his canvases, allowing his intuition, and chance, to determine where and how the paint should fall. In this way he believed that painting could express the subconscious ideas of the mind. Since the paintings did not represent anything seen or observed they could be described as **abstract**, and since they also reflected or expressed the artist's intuitive feelings they were labelled as works of **Abstract Expressionism** by the critics.

This type of action painting appealed to Gillian Ayres. She began working on a large scale on canvas pinned to the wall or stretched out on the floor of her studio. As she applied paint in sweeping brush strokes, dashes and splashes, she was aware that the painting seemed to develop a distinct personality of its own. She, of course, controlled the marks made on the canvas, but could not predict the final outcome.

145

The speed with which paint was applied – for example, fast and spontaneous or slow and deliberate – could create exciting contrasting rhythms, which she wished to exploit. Gillian Ayres seeks to achieve, however, a fine balance between energetic chaos and calm order. While delighting in the juicy rough surfaces which her layering of colours produces, she takes great care to avoid muddiness. As a result her colours retain a richness and exuberance in keeping with her belief that the network of paint on canvas parallels the richness of nature.

Among the **Old Masters** Ayres admires are works by Monet and Matisse, the 16th-century Venetian artists Titian and Veronese, and the 17th-century Flemish artist Rubens. Some of the most famous paintings of these older artists are of mythological subjects which often inspire the titles of Gillian Ayres's own work. She does not give a painting a title until it is finished. This ensures that the title reflects appropriately the character and mood of the completed piece. The title of this painting is 'Chanticlear', a play on the word chanticleer (meaning cockerel) and the character in the medieval tale of *Reynard the Fox*. Certainly the rich colours and vibrant rhythms evoke colourful feathers and distinctive sounds. In fact the French origin of the word chanticleer, from *chanter*: to sing, and *cler*: clear, encourages the association of the word with sound and in this case, the association of sound with colour.

Discussion

1.   Ask some general questions to begin with (children will probably need very little prompting to say exactly what their first impressions of this picture are): What does this picture look like? Does this picture remind you of anything? Do you like this picture? Why/why not? (The responses will vary but may be on the whole rather resistant to this type of painting which has apparently little to do with anything recognisable and seems very messy.)

2.   Talk about how big this picture is (in fact you could measure it out or estimate it as a group), then ask the children whether they would like to paint a picture like this. The idea of painting like this is often received more enthusiastically than the painting itself. Where do the children think the artist painted this picture: on an easel, on the wall, or on the floor of her studio? What arm movement (or actions) would be used to make these kind of marks in paint? How could they be described (i.e. the marks)? Do the children think some of them could have been made accidentally? (The artist enjoyed the idea of chance playing a role in the painting.) Do they think that they were all made with one paint brush? Why not? Do they think the paint has been put on thinly or thickly, smoothly or roughly?

3.   Encourage the children to look closely at the colours. How can they tell that some colours were painted over others? How many different colours has the artist used? Ask the children to think of their favourite colours for a moment. Are there colours that they like for different reasons, perhaps suited to different moods? What do the colours in this picture make them think of? What words (adjectives) would they use to describe them? Are any of the words connected with sounds, musical or natural? Could any of the words they used to describe the marks be connected with sounds? Or what sounds could they make to describe the action of painting? Ask the children why they think the artist called this picture 'Chanticlear' (some help with the meaning and origins of the word would probably be required here).

146

4. Discuss whether this would be a difficult picture to paint. Why? (Remember that it would be very easy to end up with lots of muddy colours.)

5. The picture is square – try looking at it different ways up. Do the children think it looks better any other way up? How do they think the artist decided which should be the top and bottom of the picture? Emphasise that paintings like this do not describe things you can see but perhaps things that you think about or feel, e.g. emotions and moods.

6. While looking at the picture ask the children whether their reactions to it have changed? If so, in what way?

Practical activities

1. Work on a square piece of paper and paint a picture to express your mood. Choose colours that describe how you feel and try different ways of applying paint so that your actions express your mood too. Remember that you are not painting a **portrait**, so the picture is not about your appearance but about what people cannot see. Try and suggest different moods in different pictures.

2. Take a paint brush for an outing on a large piece of paper. Try out different ways of making marks with the paint. Perhaps you could tell a story in the process. What would you do if you were the paint brush and could do whatever you felt like on the paper? Gillian Ayres uses oil paint on canvas. Other types of paint can be used with paper (see the section on materials in Chapter 4).

3. Paint a picture to complement a piece of music you have listened to. Choose colours and ways of applying paint to suggest different notes and passages in the piece, for example loud notes, soft notes, high notes, deep notes, plucked strings, bowed or strummed strings etc. This could be done in groups: each group could listen to a different piece of music and produce a painting to complement it. Then the whole class could decide which pieces of music should be played with which paintings.

4. Read the story of *Reynard the Fox* and paint a picture to suggest one of the characters in it. It could be your own version of Chanticleer or perhaps Reynard himself.

5. Choose another animal and paint a picture to suggest the animal's colouring, characteristics and sounds.

Cross refer to abstract or 'painterly' paintings: Miro's 'The Red Sun' (Picture 32), Morisot's 'Summer's Day' (Picture 25), Cézanne's 'Pommes Vertes' (Picture 34), Sargent's 'Carnation, Lily, Lily, Rose' (Picture 30) and Constable's 'Cloud Studies' (Pictures 16 and 17).

Cross refer to pictures with movement and sounds suggested: Hokusai's 'Wild Sea at Chōshi' (Picture 26), Martin's 'The Bard' (Picture 8), Gilbert and George's 'Weather Window' (Picture 37) and Blake's 'The Tyger' (Picture 22).

6. Use this work as the trigger for a series of more abstract experiments with paint itself. The starting point could be some very simple, diagrammatic images which would provide an underlying structure on which to base your experiment. You could work with colours based around a pair of **complementary colours** such as yellow and purple and make abstract works in which you try to set up a balance between the two. (Refer to Picture 30 for more details about complementary colours.)

RECORD SHEET (KEY STAGE TWO)

Name _____

Year _____

Attainment Target 1	Project 1	Teacher's Comments	Project 2	Teacher's Comments	Project 3	Teacher's Comments
● Developing ideas into finished work						
● Materials/tools used Techniques/skills						
● Context or work ● Reviewing/modifying work ● Group or individual?						
● Key elements: use of colour, shape, form, space, line, tone, pattern, texture						

Attainment Target 2	Discussion Focus	Teacher's comments
● Identifying different kinds of art and their purposes		
● Investigating characteristics of different kinds of art		
● Developing appropriate vocabulary		
● Relating artist's work to their own		

Making a Casket

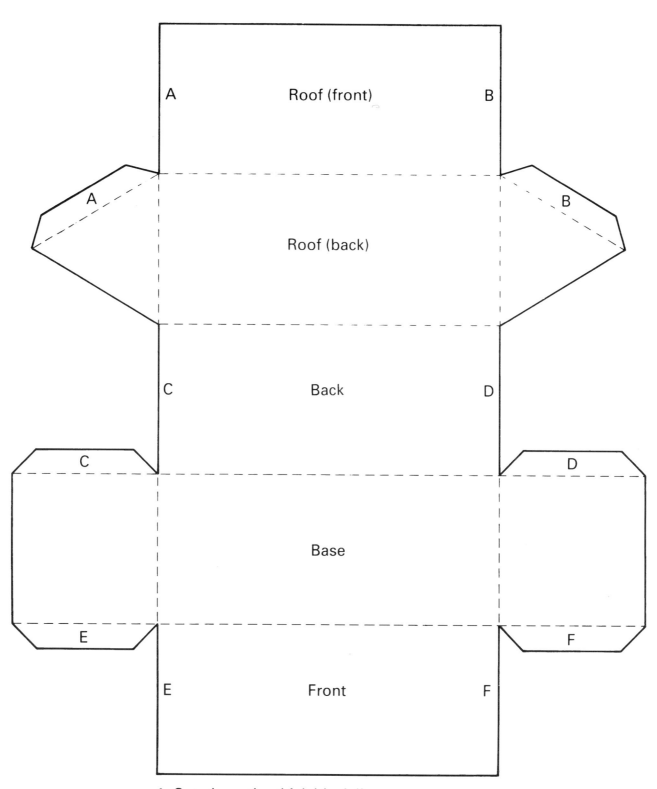

1. Cut along the thick black lines.
2. Fold along the dotted lines.
3. Stick together the areas with matching labels.

Picture Frame

Jan van Eyck's Signature

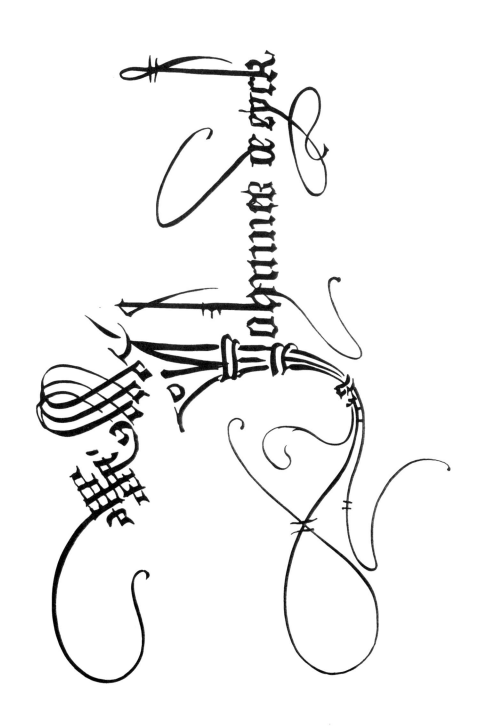

Anamorphic Projections

Anamorphic Projections

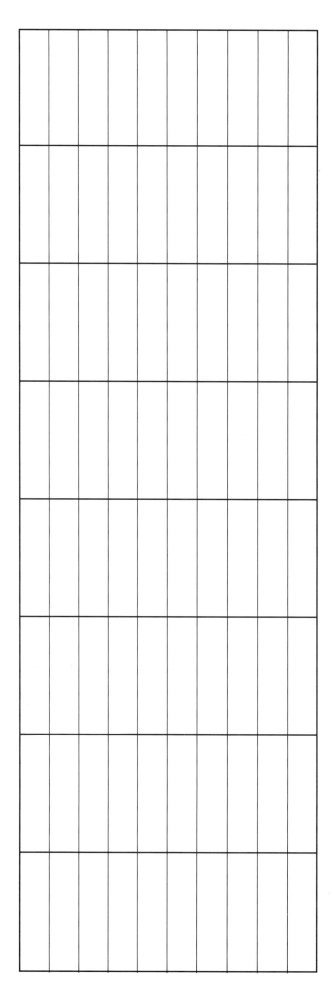

Vermeer's 'Kitchenmaid'

The Tiger

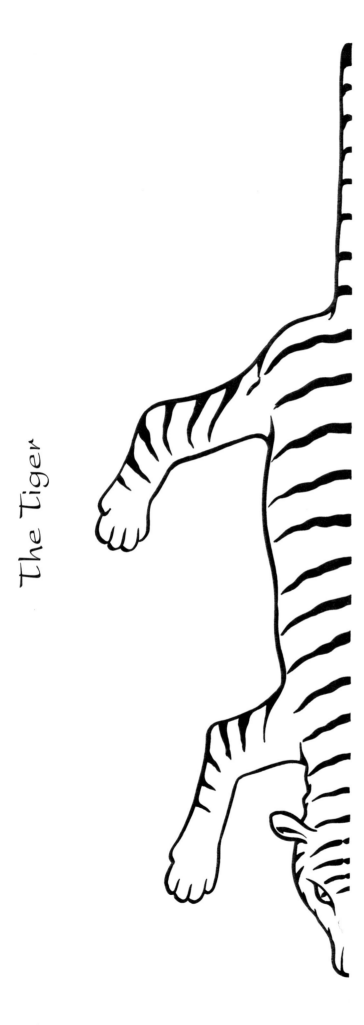

Colour Wheel

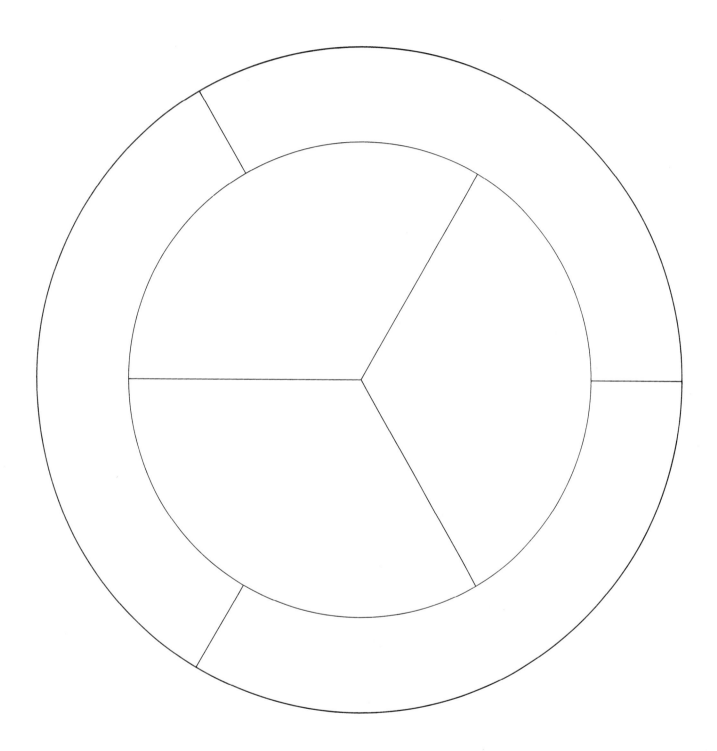

Crab/Frog

Calligraphy: Italic

a b c d e f g h i j k l m n
o p q r s t u v w x y z

A B C D E F G H I J K L M N
O P Q R S T U V W X Y Z

Calligraphy: Uncial

abcdefgh
ijklmno
pqrstuvw
xyz